The Eclipse of Man and Nature

D1598503

PHILIP SHERRARD

The Eclipse of Man
and Nature

*An Enquiry into the
Origins and Consequences
of Modern Science*

INNER TRADITIONS
LINDISFARNE PRESS

An Inner Traditions/Lindisfarne Press Book

Published by the Lindisfarne Press, P.O. BOX
127, West Stockbridge, MA 01266. Distributed
to the book trade by Inner Traditions
International. All trade inquiries should be
addressed to Inner Traditions International,
Park Street, Rochester, Vermont 05767

Library of Congress Cataloging-in-Publication Data

Sherrard, Philip
The eclipse of man and nature

Includes bibliographical references.
1. Religion and science—1946-   . 2. Man
(Christian theology)   3. Science—Philosophy
I. Title
BL256.S54 1987   261.5′5   87-2715
ISBN 0-89281-076-9 (pbk.)

Printed in the United Kingdom

AUTHOR'S NOTE

Chapters 1-3 of this book are based on the Frederick Denison Maurice lectures given at King's College, University of London in October 1975. An earlier version of Chapter 4 appeared in vol. 10 of *Studies in Church History*, ed. Derek Parker (Oxford, 1973), pp 1-20, and is published here in its revised form by kind permission of the Ecclesiastical History Society.

CONTENTS

Foreword

TWO THINGS should perhaps be said by way of a foreword to this enquiry. The first is that the enquiry itself—or evaluation—is very much confined to the world of European thought and practice. It takes its norms from this world and traces the effects of deviating from them also within this world. That is to say there is virtually no reference to the thought-forms of other cultures and traditions, such as those of Islam, or India, or the Far East. This may give the impression that the book has little to say of any significance to those living within these latter cultures and traditions, and that whatever interest it has is of concern only to Europeans or at least to those living within what we call the western world.

I do not believe this to be the case. Modern science is now a world-wide phenomenon, and it has radically altered, even indeed threatens totally to displace, the patterns of life and the values which until its advent had characterized not only the civilization of Europe and America but every other civilization as well. Yet at the same time it is a phenomenon which first manifested itself in changes of thought that took place in the European intellectual world. This is to say that it is a phenomenon which can be truly understood and evaluated only when these changes and their significance have been properly grasped. It is thus impossible to assess the essential nature of modern science except by studying it within the context of the European thought-world which constitutes its matrix and from which it emerged. And this is something that applies just as much for those who belong to non-European cultures and traditions as it does for Europeans.

Indeed, in a certain sense it is something that applies even more for those of non-European, or non-western, cultures and traditions. Modern science, in terms of its intellectual or philosophical presuppositions, is, as we noted, basically a European phenomenon; and Europeans themselves cannot but be aware that its ascendancy has in fact gone hand in hand with the disruption of the spiritual universe which gave their civilization its coherence, beauty and richness. They cannot but be aware therefore that there is an irreconcilable incompatibility between the norms of this spiritual universe and the norms of modern science. Non-Europeans may be much less aware of this. They have accepted modern science in so to speak a ready-made form, as something imported from without and whose mastery and manipulation can produce certain effects in the practical sphere without them having to bother about its intellectual premisses and whether or not these are compatible with their traditional values and patterns of life.

In this way they have been perhaps more vulnerable even than Europeans themselves, in that they have been more easily induced to believe that the acceptance of the methodology and techniques of modern science does not lead inevitably to the disruption of the spiritual universe to which their own civilizations owe all that is sacred and human about them. They have been lulled into a state of passive acquiescence to what is really a western imperialism of a far more vicious and totalitarian nature than they have ever experienced in any other form; and they have allowed themselves to be thus subjected ultimately because they have not realized that modern science will slowly but surely bring about changes in thought and action in their own worlds similar to those it has already brought about in the western world. And the only way in which they can become aware of why this is the case is by becoming conscious of the nature and implications of these changes, something which itself can only happen when they study them within the context of the European thought-world which gave modern science its birth and defined its character.

The second thing to be said is that a book which attempts to explore and evaluate the origins and consequences of modern science but is written by someone who cannot lay claim to more than the most rudimentary scientific knowledge, if even that, might well be regarded as a non-starter. Surely, it might be said, such a book can be written only by a scientist. Again, I do not believe this to be the case. Modern science has emerged because, knowingly or unknowingly, scientists themselves have accepted and continue to work within a certain framework of metaphysical or philosophical principles that constitute a reality in their own right and quite apart from the phenomenon to which they have given birth. This is to say that modern science, far from being merely a pragmatic, materialist or empirical discipline independent of metaphysics—and it is this which many scientist would like us to believe—in fact presupposes and implements in its every aspect, theoretical and practical, a metaphysical or philosophical view of things that is anything but neutral, self-evident, self-proven or a matter of common sense. It is this view that determines the whole character of modern science as well as the character of the society which is fashioned in its image.

Few contemporary scientists appear to be aware of this. Scientists are specialists, and within the confines of their specialities they are no doubt capable of producing theories and effects consistent with the premises they have adopted. But scientific knowledge itself has no depth and no complexity: it represents the lowest common denominator of the most average kind of mentality. Its authors have never even grasped the crucial distinction between wisdom and speculative hypothesis based on experiment. Hence once they venture outside the confines of their specialities and try to justify their theories and effects in terms of value or to assess their metaphysical or human significance, they produce only nonsense, because the premises which they take as their standards are not comprehensive enough to allow them to do anything else.

Indeed, judged by the normal standards of metaphysical or philosophical discourse, scientists—but for the most rare exceptions—display a total lack of competence in this realm: the thought in this respect of such a highly esteemed scientist as Albert Einstein, for instance, is bewildering in its naivity. Perhaps the reason for this is not far to seek. Distinction in any field of modern science presupposes the mastery of such a vast amount of sheer technical—mathematical and mechanical—information and expertise that the aspiring scientist is compelled to devote, virtually exclusively, the long years stretching between the latter half of his secondary schooling and the termination of his undergraduate and graduate studies to acquiring it. This means that he has little or no time during these crucial formative years—and in all likelihood scarcely more time during his subsequent professional life—to devote himself to the pursuit of an entirely different order of knowledge, that precisely which pertains to the world of ideas—or metaphysical and philosophical principles—by which none the less his own thought and practice as a scientist are determined at every step. Access to this world in its turn presupposes at least as great a degree of assiduous study, over at least an equal number of years, as the mastery of the mathematical and related technical knowledge needed to be a scientist.

This is too often forgotten, or not taken into account. In fact, while it is entirely recognized that in order to be a scientist—or a musician, or a ballet-dancer, or even an international football player—these long years of study and practice are a prerequisite, it is somehow tacitly assumed that the capacity to think coherently, and to set down one's thought cogently, does not require much training but is the automatic prerogative of whoever is proficient in any other profession or skill. That this, alas, is far from being the case is demonstrated only too clearly, as I have already noted, when scientists venture beyond the confines of their specialities into the metaphysical or philosophical realm. Moreover, the pursuit of technical knowledge to the degree which is needed in order to attain proficiency in any branch of modern science blunts, if it does not atrophy, the capacity to enter that realm at all. Scientists themselves are protected against becoming aware of this because they have ensconced themselves within the departmental structure of modern schools and universities where, unmolested by any concern for values, rights and meanings, they are free to build the New World of which they—along with their clients, the corporate industrialists and the big-businessmen—are the self-elected ruling class.

Thus it is practically inevitable that the task of elucidating the intellectual origins of modern science and the metaphysical ideas that it presupposes, as well as of assessing the consequences, in human and other terms, of their implementation, has to be undertaken by a non-scientist, for the scientist is unlikely to possess the qualifications needed in order to undertake it. This is not to say that I myself do possess these qualifications in a definitive sense—I am only too aware of my shortcomings in this respect. But it is to say that I recognize the terms in which alone such a task has to be undertaken if it is to serve any useful purpose, and that I have tried to write this book in accordance with them. I hope that as a result it may at least be of some assistance to whoever is concerned to understand how and why we find ourselves today in a world in which it is increasingly difficult to live as a human being.

Katounia, Limni, Evia.
Summer 1986

I

The Human Image

THE MAIN PURPOSE of this short book is twofold. It is to show, first, how the worldview of modern science, which assumed a definitive shape in the seventeenth century, has its roots in certain prior developments in Christian theology that partially eclipsed the full Christian understanding of man and his destiny; and, second, how the acceptance and implementation of this scientific worldview have resulted in an ever-accelerating dehumanization of man and of the forms of his society, with all the repercussions that this has had, and is still having, in the realm of nature. But neither of these two interrelated themes can be discussed with any fruitfulness unless we already possess a clear idea of what is meant by the full Christian understanding of man. Before we can describe a deviation, we must first establish the norm. In other words, our enquiry must begin with anthropology. It must begin with an attempt to establish who man is according to the deepest insights of the Christian tradition.

This, however, at once calls for two preliminary explanations. In the first place, why is the norm for the understanding of who man is to be taken from the Christian tradition and not from somewhere else? Even granted that certain developments in Christian theology prepared the ground for the emergence of the kind of materialistic philosophy whose implementation in practical terms has crippled so much human and other life, this does not mean that Christianity itself ever possessed a satisfactory understanding of man and his destiny, least of all one that can stand as a norm against which the value of other ideas about who man is can be assessed. Might not, for instance, the

Platonic understanding of man, or that of a non-Christian religion like Islam, be more adequate? Why, indeed, does our understanding of man have to presuppose the recognition of religious or supra-human and metaphysical principles at all?

One cannot answer such questions without stepping over into the sphere of personal commitment and belief. To start with, then, I take it as axiomatic that man is in essence a spiritual being whose nature and destiny can be fulfilled only through the realization of potentialities of a kind that lies far beyond anything that falls within the sphere of physical, biological, psychological or sociological explanation or cognizance. This means that he is a being whose essential qualities cannot be grasped by the human mind working within the limits of rational, psychological or sensory perception.

Hence if he is to be understood at all it can only be in the light of a wisdom or gnosis that pertains to a spiritual or metaphysical order—a wisdom or gnosis that has been made known to man through divine revelation and whose *a priori* acceptance by man is a necessary condition of his attaining any non-spurious knowledge not just of human but of all forms of reality. As a wisdom of this kind is to be found only in a religious or spiritual tradition, it follows that it is to the principles of such a tradition that one must turn for an anthropology that does some kind of justice to man's true nature.

Why, though, turn, as in the present case, to the Christian tradition? I suppose the answer to this is the purely pragmatic one that Christianity is the only authentic living religious tradition which we who belong to the cultural orbit of the European world possess—the only religious tradition which, in spite of everything, is still capable of nourishing and maturing our spiritual life, whether individual or collective. I do not mean by this that no one belonging to what I have called the cultural orbit of the European world can find a spiritual home in a non-Christian religion. That is not the case at all, and there are individuals who have done precisely this. But they are exceptions that prove the rule, for it involves the crossing of a cultural and above all psychological barrier in a way which few can accomplish without serious inner dislocation and disharmony. Consequently, if in purely practical terms, whether personal or social—and they must be personal before they can be social—there is to be any stemming, let alone turning, of the tide of progressive materialization and disintegration on which we are all now carried, it can only be, except for the few of whom we have spoken, through the re-affirmation of Christian norms. Hence it is important to know what in the fullest sense constitutes these norms.

Yet to speak of reaffirming Christian norms in the fullest sense is to beg an enormous question, one that brings me to my second preliminary explanation. For where in fact are these norms to be found? Quite clearly, there is no unanimous Christian answer, for if there were Christendom itself would not be divided into several dissenting and often fractious groups, acknowledging no common body of doctrine and each appealing to its own theological authorities. Thus, anyone who attemps to discuss any theme in the light of Christian principles must begin by specifying the pedigree of these principles, by specifying what particular doctrinal authorities he acknowledges. Otherwise he is in danger of confusing the issue and of exposing himself to the charge of misrepresentation on the part of those whose allegiance lies elsewhere.

This being the case, I should make it clear from the start that my own version of Christian anthropology derives above all from the Greek patristic theological tradition; and if I were asked to exemplify more specifically I would single out for particular reference the works of St Maximos the Confessor (c.580-662).[1] Of course, St Maximos's theology itself presupposes the work of his great predecessors, and in particular that of the Cappadocian Fathers (fourth century) and the writings (fifth century) attributed to St Dionysios the Areopagite. Moreover, it is also inherent in his successors within the Orthodox Christian tradition—and here one may specify above all the works of St Symeon the New Theologian (949-1022) and St Gregory Palamas (c.1296-1359), although it must by no means be assumed that the tradition stops here and does not continue down to the present day.[2]

Unfortunately, the same cannot be said where the Roman Catholic and Protestant traditions are concerned, for although there are deep affinities between the Greek patristic theologians and Latin theologians such as John Scotus Erigena (c.810-c.877), William of St-Thierry (c.1085-1148) and Meister Eckhart (c.1260-1377), in the main, in a manner that will be discussed in the second chapter of this book, the Roman Catholic and Protestant traditions became dominated by other standards, with consequences that have been disastrous in all spheres of human and other life. This is not to claim that the understanding and insights of, say, a St Maximos the Confessor have been totally lost within these traditions; but in so far as they have been expressed they are to be found more in the works of mystics like Jan Van Ruysbroeck (1293-1381), Angelus Silesius (1624-77), the Cambridge Platonists (seventeenth century) or of poets like William Blake and W. B. Yeats, than in the works of formal Christian theologians.

What, then, is this understanding of man and his destiny according to the doctrinal masters of the tradition which I have specified? Here the starting-point of our enquiry must be Christology—the understanding of the relationship between the divine and the human in the person of Christ. That is why Christology is such an important theme within the Christian tradition, for any shift in Christological interpretation will have repercussions in all other spheres of Christian interpretation.

Thus, for instance, the extreme form of the old Nestorian Christology so prevalent in our times—the notion, which lies concealed within so much western theology, that Christ is only a man, albeit a very good man, a man intensely conscious of God—destroys the full understanding of man proposed by the doctrinal masters we have here invoked just as decisively today as it did in the fifth century. For the understanding of our doctrinal masters stands or falls on the recognition of the divine humanity of Christ, of His divine-human complexity or God-manhood.

It is the idea of this divine humanity that establishes the norm for man. Christ—our idea of Christ—is the model by reference to which we can answer the question about who we are. He is *the* man, 'the first-born of every creature',[4] the archetype of which every man is, in terms of his potentialities, the image. Thus what we are at any given moment—our personality—is what we are able to realize of the infinite potentialities which our divine-human nature contains within its depths, attending their fulfilment.

This may appear strange to us. We have become so used to regarding Christ as a kind of unique exception, someone who appeared, in an inimitable once-and-for-all manner, at a certain time in history, that we tend to consider Him as someone so essentially different from us that He cannot serve as a model of what we ourselves have it in us to become. This attitude in its turn has tended to obscure two equally important truths for us.

The first is that this divine humanity of Christ—His God-manhood—is not something that He acquires by virtue of the historical Incarnation alone. From the first He is *the* man, 'the first-born of every creature'. This is to say that the Christological ideas that apply to the incarnate Christ apply first of all to the eternal being of Christ and are but revealed in the historical Incarnation. This of course is the same where all aspects of Christian doctrine are concerned: they all apply primarily to eternal truths, not to historical events, for every historical event has its origin or prototype on the plane of metahistory, and is of significance only in so far as it is seen in relationship to this prototype. That is why those Christians who assert that what makes their religion unique is that it is based on a historical fact are guilty of a certain naivity.

The second important truth which has tended to be obscured for us and which we must assimilate if we wish to grasp the full sense of how Christ may serve as a model for what we can become may be stated in this form: that what Christ is by nature we are by derivation, by divine filiation. It is because Christ is the Son of God who is also man that we are sons of God. The difference between Christ and us is that He is eternally God's Son, while we are God's sons because we are created in the image of Christ's divine humanity, His God-manhood. The sonship of Christ is the type and ground of the relation in which the human stands to the divine. In Christ, who is the original man, the type of creation, men are created to be the sons of God. And to be a son of God is to have the divine as the determining element of our being. It is for God to be, in an active and not merely in a passive manner, the source, the inmost centre of our reality.

Yet if God is the inmost centre of our reality, we also are examples of God-manhood. In fact, it is precisely this that makes us human and that constitutes our humanity. To the degree to which we fail to attain a full realization of this we also fail to be human. The idea that man can be human apart from God is a false idea: it is the return of the Nestorian heresy in another form. The very concept of man implies a relationship, a connection with God. Where one affirms man one also affirms God, and where one affirms God one also affirms man. Although man may—and does—deny his relationship with God, he cannot escape from it because it is written into his very existence: his existence as such presupposes it, and without it he would quite simply not exist. Correspondingly, God cannot escape from His relationship with man because that, too, is written into His very existence. That is why Christ is the model of our humanity. That is why our understanding of who man is must, in the Christian perspective, depend on our understanding of who Christ is.

However, before this Christology is discussed, a few words should be said about two apparently antagonistic ways of envisaging the relationship between God and man—ways which are reconciled in the idea of God-manhood itself and which therefore represent a kind of false dilemma which the Christology of our doctrinal masters resolves. The first of these ways of envisaging the relationship between God and man is that associated with the Old Testament. According to this way, God absolutely transcends man; there is an absolute separateness and heterogeneity between them; and man sees himself as an insignificant creature whose life can achieve positive content only on condition that he submits himself without reserve to the autocratic, unlimited and overwhelming majesty that rules the world and that issues appropriate commands for its good governance. God and man in this view constitute two distinct ontological realities, and between them there is no real kinship or inner identity. As created in the image of God, man is essentially and qualitatively different from his archetype. He is a derivative and dependent creature, impotent to save himself from his own nothingness and from the tragic dereliction of his life upon earth. Except in the case of Enoch and Elijah, there is no suggestion in the Old Testament that man either does or should actually go to heaven.

I said that this way of envisaging the relationship between God and man is that associated with the Old Testament because what it probably represents is less the Old Testament as such than the reading of it, practised, for instance, by the Reformers when they 'rediscovered' it in the sixteenth and seventeenth centuries, which takes little, or no account of the oral tradition of Judaism according to which the formal skeleton of the written Pentateuch was given its living, inner and organic interpretation. In any case, this conception of the relationship between God and man is modified by the prophets, for here it is no longer seen as based on blind fear before a despotic and arbitrary master. The element of love enters in, and the kind of fear which is not abject terror but the voice of conscience and the dread of contaminating what is holy, of soiling what is or should be pure. Moreover, the humility and the self-surrender which the sense of the imponderable otherness of God engenders are qualities without which all relationships of genuine love are impossible; and they constitute something very different from compulsory obedience.

Yet whatever its connection with the Old Testament, there is no doubt that this idea of God's omnipotence and man's powerlessness has penetrated deeply into the Christian tradition, especially—but by no means exclusively—in its western form. Here no less a figure that St Augustine is crucial.[5] It is one of the paradoxes, and also one of the tragedies, of the western Christian tradition that the man who affirmed so strongly the presence of God in the depths of his own self, and so the ultimate independence of the human personality from all worldly categories, should as a dogmatic theologian have been responsible more perhaps than any other Christian writer for 'consecrating' within the Christian world the idea of man's slavery and impotence due to the radical perversion of human nature through original sin. It has been St Augustine's theology which in the West has veiled down to the present day the full radiance of the Christian revelation of divine sonship— the full revelation of who man essentially is.[6]

St Augustine's theology in this respect was formulated above all in his struggle against Pelagianism. Pelagianism is a tendency to go to the other extreme and to affirm man's being as a reality external to and independent of God—a kind of equal partner in the God-man relationship, endowed with his own self-sufficient will which meets and interacts with that of God in a cooperation which places man on the same level as God. St Augustine was quite right to see that implicit in such an assumption was that act of rebellion against God which has characterized so much of the non-religious humanism of modern times: the idea that in the end man is self-determining and has no need of God, the idea of man's self-deification.

It was in the face of this implication that St Augustine insisted on the transcendence of the divine. But so anxious was he to forestall the growth of the idea of man as a self-subsistent entity that he practically denied him all positive reality whatsoever: he is merely the slave of the congenital principle of sin, the depraved creature of a transcendent God whose nature is totally other than his own and who may, through filling man's emptiness with an external gift of grace, save him from damnation if He so wills.

St Augustine does not of course go so far as to deny all reality to man: to do that would be to deny at the same time the total difference between Creator and creature and so, by a kind of inversion, to conclude in what virtually amounts to a pantheism, in the idea that everything is in its own right divine. But he does appear to deny that man possesses any creative free will and so any possibility of a dynamic relationship with the divine in which he—man—is an active spiritual partner. He deprives the element of manhood in the God-manhood reality of any genuine positive quality, and to do this is to empty the concept of divine sonship of its effective significance.

This concept can in fact only have effective significance so long as it is understood that man is not merely other than God, irreducibly alien to God, but is on the contrary the specific expression of God's creative energy and participates in this energy as a condition of having any existence whatsoever. Grace, that is to say, is not something extrinsic, not something added to man's nature; it is inherent in the conditions of his birth. In other words, one could say that the absolute gulf between Creator and creature, and the total transcendence of God which constitutes that gulf, are themselves transcended in the very act of creation. Creation presents this paradox: that it affirms a spanless abyss between God and creature which the act of creation itself bridges.

What is in question here is of course the immanence of the divine in creation and particularly in man. This introduces the second of those two ways of envisaging the relationship between God and man and is the other pole, so to speak, of the concept of divine transcendence, both poles being brought together in the unity of the God-manhood. More will be said of this later. Here it is relevant to note that if the Old Testament stresses the absolute transcendence of God (however much this may be modified in the ways we have indicated), the idea of divine immanence—of the indwelling of God in the creature— is foreshadowed more explicitly in classical Greek thought, particularly of course in Platonic thought.

Briefly, Platonic thought envisages reality as a structure of different levels descending from the realm of intelligible Ideas,[7] or archetypes, down to the least particle of sensible or material existence, from the highest forms of being to the lowest. In this structure, every form of being that exists on the sensible or material plane is seen as having its origin in its corresponding archetypal Idea in the intelligible realm: it is an image of this archetype. This is to say that every sensible form represents both an unfolding and a greater degree of condensation or materialization of its archetype; or, to put this the other way round, the archetype contains and embraces the sensible form in its intelligible or spiritual state.

Such a conception of the immanence of the transcendent archetype in its sensible counterpart, or of the indwelling of the sensible form in its intelligible archetype, is expressed in terms of the participation of the one in the other. The sensible image does not simply reflect the archetype on an inferior level: it actually participates in the transcendent reality of the archetype. There is a relationship between archetype and image, model and likeness, that goes beyond that of mere external copying and implies a real kinship or affinity between them. In some sense, the image is the archetype in another mode, and only differs from the archetype because the conditions in which it is manifested impose on it a different form.

Essentially therefore the principle is one of transformation of inner into outer, of an interlocking scale of modalities in which the same basic theme is repeated. The Platonic universe is really a hierarchy of images, all co-existing, each issuing from and sharing in the one above it, from the highest supra-essential realities down to those of the visible world. It is this structure of participation which constitutes the great golden chain of being, that unbroken connection between the highest and the lowest, heaven and earth. In this structure there is nothing that is not animate, nothing that is mere dead matter. All is endowed with being, all—even the least particle—belongs to a living trans-muting whole. Each thing is the revelation of the indwelling creative spirit. And it was against this background of Platonic understanding about how the image participates in the arche-type that the conception of man as created in the image of God received a new and more positive content in the Christian idea of God-manhood.

This idea of God-manhood was the subject of profound meditation over the first Christian centuries; and certain crys-tallizations of this meditation appear in the formulas of the Council of Chalcedon (451), above all in the famous statement that the two natures—the divine and the human—are united in Christ 'without division or confusion'. They appear, too, in the works of the Greek Fathers to whom I have referred above.[8] Here, then, we are at the threshold of our enquiry.

The understanding of these theologians in relationship to this theme has its starting-point in a certain actuality, metaphysical before it is historical, supra-temporal before it is temporal. This actuality expresses itself in the affirmation that in Christ God is man. What does this mean? In what sense is God man in the person of Christ? What is this Christic mystery? In some way, the divine is joined to the human. But in what way? It is not sufficient to say that the two natures are merely juxtaposed, for that would be to imply that there is no real union, only a temporary compact which can be dissolved, the elements form-ing it then falling apart again and being separated. The union of the two natures—the divine and the human—is consummated in Christ in such a way that the elements composing it are inseparable, and this means that the human element, including the body, is indissolubly one with God's eternal nature. This is to say that there is not only a divine penetration into the realm of the human; there is also a human penetration into the realm of the divine. The union of the two natures in Christ, in other words, is a two-way affair, or has two complementary aspects: it is a 'humanization' of God which is simultaneously a divinization of man or, to adapt the words of Herakleitos, in Christ the divine is human, the human is divine.

This is the crux of the mystery; and to express it in any terms which do not take adequate account of this dual and reciprocal movement and relationship is to obscure its full significance. The union of the two natures in Christ is so intimate that 'either is the other's mine', and yet in spite of this intimacy each nature keeps its own integral identity. This means that in becoming human God is fulfilling a potentiality in His own nature as such, while in becoming divine the human is fulfilling a pontentiality which is fully in accord with human nature as such.

Moreover, the divine can only fulfil this potentiality in union with the human, just as the human can only fulfil it in union with the divine. The union of the two natures in Christ is therefore based on a certain inherent polarity between the divine and the human. God and man are in some sense exemplars or paradigms of one another, to such an extent that the qualities possessed by the one may also be possessed by the other. The humanization of God and the deification of man condition each other mutually, for the simple reason that they express a tendency inherent in the nature of each which can be realized only through a mutual self-giving of what each is to the other; and yet, it must be repeated, this self-giving does not mean any loss or confusion of identity: the duality of the two natures and their qualities are preserved within the unity.

The word which perhaps most fully conveys the degree of reciprocity involved in the idea of Christ's divine humanity is the Greek word *perichoresis*—a word which expresses the dynamic co-penetration of the uncreated and the created, the divine and the human, and so something more than is implied by the phrase, *communicatio idiomatum*, with which it is sometimes equated. Fundamentally, Christ substantiates such a *perichoresis*: the synthesis of two natures or two substances each with its individual qualities to form a single person or hypostasis who is, as it were, the perfection of both. What is formed in this union is not of course a new nature, but rather a new mode of activity for the two natures. In virtue of their union, a new mode of activity emerges—a divine-human or theandric mode. It is a mode in which God acts in a human manner and in which man acts in a divine manner; in which the divine energy is humanized and the human energy is divinized. In other words, in the hypostatic union—this union of the two natures in Christ—the boundaries of the natural modes of activity and even of existence of each of the unified elements is transcended in this new and more perfect mode—although as the union itself is fully in accord with tendencies inherent in each of the elements this new mode of activity or existence may also be described as natural to each.

Yet this new theandric energy or theandric activity is not merely a mixture of the two modes of activity proper to each of the elements. It is a co-operation of these two modes—a co-operation of the divine and the human energies. The identity of the two elements remains intact. But it is through their co-operation that this identity is developed and even perfected. The human energy cannot develop or perfect its potentiality without the divine, or the divine without the human. As already emphasized, the humanization of God is fully in accord with the divine nature as such. It is not something consummated in view of the specific conditions to which humanity was reduced as a result of the Fall. The humanization—or enhumaniza-tion—of God is a reality which in itself is independent of the Fall, although of course the Fall crucially influences the manner in which it is revealed in the historical Incarnation. God's transcending of His own transcendence in an outgoingness through which He becomes immanent in His creation may from one point of view represent a limitation of the divine; but from another and more important point of view it is an act of creative self-expression without which the divine itself would remain incomplete. There is a divine as well as a human form of ecstasy.

The person of Christ is unique. The hypostasis of Christ is unique. But what Christ is by nature—this divine-human reality whose subject is the Logos of God—man is by filiation, by participation. This is the image, as it were, in which man is created. Man is a creature created to be the son of God. He is born to be free of the sphere of death and corruption. Death and corruption are profoundly alien to his nature; they are profoundly unnatural to him. What is natural to him is precisely that eternal life which is his through participation in the divine. This deification of man is realized only in relationship to that unique divine-human reality who is Christ. Human nature with its energy and will is fulfilled in synthetic union with the divine nature in Christ and is enhypostasized there. It is enhypostasized there on the model of the hypostatic union of the divine and the human in Christ.

There is a co-operation of the divine and the human, the uncreated and the created. Christ is the perfect man, the complete man, the whole man. But Christ is also God. This is to say that, paradox as it may sound, it is God alone who is the perfect man. Only God is completely and utterly human. As we said, in so far as man fails to realize the divine in himself, to that extent he falls short of being completely human. He remains less than human. His human nature is truncated just as the divine nature is truncated and less than divine if it is not humanized. It is not accidental or a cause of surprise that man's attempts to be only human—to fulfil the ideals of the non-religious humanism of the last centuries—results in a dehumanization both of man and of the forms of the society which he has fabricated around himself.

Again it must be stressed that this desire and capacity of man to transcend the limits of his psycho-physical or his created nature, and so to actualize his divine or his uncreated nature, are not something added to his nature. In fact, it is the most fundamental characteristic of his nature, and only through its realization may this nature be said to have realized its potentialities and have become what it inherently is. Not to penetrate into the realm of the divine is for human nature to be frustrated and crippled at its most real and creative centre. It is for human nature to be distorted at its roots. Man's failure to live according to a divine mode is a form of self-mutilation. And it can equally be affirmed, with the image of the person of Christ before one, that God's failure to live according to a human mode would also be a form of self-mutilation. God is always seeking to work the miracle of His incarnation in all men. But He can work this miracle only in so far as man himself will manifest Him. If it is true that without the divine dimension the human dimension would be deprived of reality, it is equally true that without the human dimension the divine would be deprived of self-manifestation. Without man, God cannot exist.

Here, then, by way of this introduction, we reach a first idea of who man is: a creature who lives through participation in the divine, and who fails to be human to the degree to which he fails to realize this participation in a fully active sense. This idea is most succinctly expressed in the concept of God-manhood, of man's divine-human complexity, to which we have already referred. As was emphasized when we spoke of the unity of the divine and the human in Christ, the elements of which this unity consist must not be regarded as two totally independent realities which are juxtaposed alongside one another and which exist separately from each other. They are distinct, but not separate—'two distincts, division none', fused but not confused. The very idea of man as such—of man as distinct from God—includes the idea of his relationship to God, just as the idea of God includes the idea of man and is intimately linked with man's experience of himself as a person. Again, it is only in so far as man fails to experience himself as a person that he will also fail to include in his idea of himself his relationship to God.[9]

This relationship is not merely an external one, between two heterogeneous and independent elements. It is one of reciprocity between elements with an inherent affinity one with the other. The very fact that it is possible to conceive of God and man at all presupposes an initial intrinsic relationship between them. It is because of this that the idea of man existing apart from God, or of God as existing apart from man, is, as we said, a false idea. If we think of God as totally and absolutely transcendent to man, and of man as without any inner affinity with God, we fail to recognize that it is man's divinity that constitutes the essence of his humanity and consequently we dehumanize our idea of man. But at the same time, if we think of this divinity as belonging to man in his own right, so to say, and not as deriving from God who is altogether 'other' than man, we end up by thinking that God is unnecessary and so by denying Him and in deifying ourselves in His place; and as our human nature cannot be completed without God—as we said, only God is fully human—to do this also means that we dehumanize our idea of man.

Both the attitude which sees God as irreducibly outside and beyond man and the attitude which attributes to man the principle of his own existence or regards him as a self-subsistent splinter of divinity result in a dehumanization of man. Only when God and man are seen as indivisible but distinct elements in a divine-human reality in which the presence of the transcendent God constitutes the core of man's being, and in which God and man mutually determine each other, is it possible to envisage either God or man in a way which perhaps does some justice to the mystery and majesty of both.

We have said that in becoming divine man fulfils a potentiality inherent in his own nature, and that in fulfilling it he transcends the limitations of his created being and penetrates into the realm of the uncreated, of the divine. We have also said that there is an affinity between God and man on the analogy of the affinity between the archetype and its image affirmed in Platonic thought; and that if God is distinct from man He is also, and simultaneously, the true creative centre of man's being. When St Paul speaks of Christ living in him,[10] what is postulated is that the seed of this realization is present from the beginning in the depths of his heart. It is ridiculous to suppose that man can have an experience of which he does not possess the possibility. But if this is the case it is equally ridiculous to suppose that the human being can be defined exclusively as a created entity, different from God in principle and absolutely separate from Him, any relationship between God and man being therefore merely extrinsic. Indeed, to argue in this way is to presume that there can be something outside the all-embracing and all-pervading reality of God.

[29]

We are confronted with a kind of duality, or double level of consciousness. On one level I recognize that as a created entity the ground of my existence is not in myself: it is outside or beyond myself, rooted in a principle other than myself. It is rooted in God. I am but derivative, and in terms of my created self I am rootless, groundless. At the same time I am also aware that there is something in me that is not rootless and groundless, something that surpasses, or lies beneath, that level of consciousness with which I normally identify myself—my rational self-consciousness; and I am also aware that this something—of which in fact most of the time I may not be aware—is the real centre of my being, is my real self, and that I am not the I of my superficial self-consciousness but I am this other deeper self: I, the real I, is this other, this mostly submerged and unheeded source of my being.

Thus for me to know myself is not to know and describe a given or objective reality. On the contrary, it is for me to make it possible for that centre of my being—the centre which constitutes my unique and personal essence and which in spite of that I cannot call *mine* or *myself*—to act and energize through me, something which it cannot do so long as I remain on the surface of things, content with my purely empirical self and its aggrandisement.

In other words, there is in man a difference between his inmost self and the self with which he usually and mistakenly identifies himself, his everyday empirical self; and it may be this split in his self-awareness, and the fact that in his outer, more superficial empirical self he is capable of ignoring and to a considerable extent of becoming impervious to his inner self, that is the most evident symptom of that internal dislocation of man's being which in the Christian tradition is indicated by the term 'Fall'.

Man is in some way double in himself. There is a Cain and an Abel in him. Indeed, the Cain in him—his superficial ego—is even capable of denying and so of metaphorically killing the real source of his being, his own inner depths, the Abel in him. He is then truly in the power of the enemy, the Evil One, Satan. Yet even such a denial is but the reverse face of the recognition

[30]

in himself of something which is the ground of his created nature and which yet cannot be completely identified with this nature: a kind of spiritual subject that gives a wholeness and a stability to his existence and is at the same time his own self at that point at which it is most genuine, creative and unique.

Platonic thought has of course always been willing to recognize a core of divinity in man, a ray emanating from the central Sun of the intelligible world, itself uncreated and divine—although it should be remembered in this connection that even in Platonic thought this divine element in man is regarded as qualitatively limited and modified and cannot simply be identified with the Deity in an absolute sense. But patristic Christian thought has been more hesitant in this respect. It has been concerned lest such a recognition should open the door to a dualism far more radical and drastic than that implied in the recognition of this split in man's awareness of himself to which I referred just now. This latter dualism—if dualism it is—is a kind of rift within man's own inner consciousness. Moreover, it is something which is in a sense unnatural, something which is the result of a certain inner dislocation or rupture, to be healed by a process of reintegration.

The dualism which patristic theologians claim that Platonic thought promotes is one that posits a clear and unbridgeable division between the intelligible and the sensible world, to such an extent that the latter—which includes the human body as well as all other physical reality—is regarded as a purely negative not to say evil category, one incapable of being penetrated by or of participating in the divine. They feel that the consequence of this is that the soul—which in Platonic thought belongs by nature to the intelligible world and so is by nature divine—is regarded as enclosed within the body as within a prison or a tomb as a punishment for some primitive evil or misdirected choice; and that the purpose of the religious life will then be seen as a catharsis which will release or deliver the entrapped soul from its prison so that it can return to its seat in the intelligible world.

Such a view virtually amounts to identifying man with his soul, itself regarded as divine by nature, and so to attributing to man as a self-sufficient independent entity the principle of his own self-divinization—a divinization to be achieved by freeing the soul from the sensible world to which the body belongs, that is to say, by abandoning the body. In the patristic view, on the other hand, man is regarded as a soul-body complex and his divinization is to be achieved not by freeing his soul from its entanglement with the body and the sensible world but by freeing his integral soul-body complex from the sphere of death and corruption into which it has fallen.

Nevertheless—because otherwise they would involve their whole doctrine in a maze of contradictions as well as deny the witness of so much Christian experience—patristic theologians do recognize the presence in man of something which, if it is not divine, is yet not un-divine; which if it is not uncreated, is yet not created. If it is a potentiality of man's nature to attain divinization—and this is central to the Christian understanding of man here envisaged—there must be in him that which is capable of apprehending the divine and penetrating into it. There must be in him a point of unity between his spirit and the Spirit of God: some organ on the borders, so to speak, of the created and the uncreated which is capable of linking both and of experiencing both. Such an organ may be 'created' in the sense that it depends on God and is not God; but it may also be termed 'uncreated' in the sense that it is not entirely other than God or entirely separate from Him: there must be some kinship or affinity between the two, for otherwise any real communion and union between them would be impossible, and the kind of experience recorded by St Paul and by countless other Christian and non-Christian saints and mystics could have no reality.

In fact it is precisely the Christian saints and mystics who most clearly affirm the presence of this spiritual subject in man, a subject that indwells in the soul and illumines the soul and yet is not simply to be identified with it. That is why short of denying the validity of the experience recorded by these most profound witnesses, Christian thinkers also must acknowledge that there is in man, at the deepest part of his being, something which is not confined to the limits of his mortal and created nature but which, transcending these limits, may derivatively participate in the eternity of God Himself. In other words, what man is in himself, in his inmost essence—that which determines and qualifies all aspects of his existence—is not temporal or relative, but eternal and absolute. Man himself may be unaware of this grace inherent in him, or he may fail to develop its potentiality—again, in our age this is the norm, not the exception. But it is present in him whether he is aware of it or not. It is, in fact, that by virtue of which alone he can achieve his humanity, or be human.

I stress this because it is in many ways the crux of what I have been saying. According to our doctrinal masters, the fundamental purpose of human life, on whose fulfilment depends the realization of the human state, is what they call man's divinization or deification. But if man is capable of 'becoming God', then there must be something in him through which he can enter into fellowship and communion with the divine, something that does not realize its own potentialities except through that fellowship and communion. There must be something in him that may know and experience spiritual or metaphysical realities, know and experience what is absolute and eternal.

This something—and here the rationalist philosophers are right—cannot be the reason. The reason can merely formulate notions and propositions. It is the systematizing faculty, combining, distinguishing, classifying according to its own logical laws and rules the forms through which it conceives material that is external to it. If the reason is the sole organ of human knowledge, then man can have no direct and immediate knowledge and experience of what is absolute and eternal. At best, if he accepts revelation, his knowledge will be but an exterior and indirect recognition of the truths it enshrines, without any possibility of direct or immediate participation in them; while if he rejects revelation, then it will be confined to the most superficial aspects of what is relative and temporal. In either case, that process of deification, on which the patristic view of our humanity depends, is effectively precluded.

Patristic theologians, however, affirm that the reason is not the sole organ or faculty of knowledge that man possesses. They affirm that he possesses, whether he is aware of it or not, whether he develops it or not, a supra-rational capacity for knowing and experiencing, a spiritual intellect as distinct from

[33]

the natural reason.[11] This spiritual intellect is, they say, the God-like faculty in man, the spirit breathed into him by the Holy Spirit in the act of his creation and that which in the deepest part of himself he is. They describe this organ or faculty as dwelling in the depths of the soul, as the eye of the soul, and as constituting the innermost aspect of the heart, man's spiritual subject or 'inner man' by means of which he is able to contemplate spiritual realities and even to attain direct union with God. As such it differs from the reason in that it does not operate by means of dissection and analysis, and it differs again from the reason in that it does not form or derive its ideas from material which is external to itself but receives them from an internal fusion with the divine Logos Himself.

These divine ideas, in the light of which the spiritual intellect knows the inner and true nature of things, are creative but uncreated ideas. Such an idea is not an abstraction, or a concept, or an analogy, drawn from an external object through logical deduction or induction. It is on the contrary the spiritual energy issuing from God according to which a thing receives its existence, an energy manifesting itself in visible form. The spiritual intellect thus knows all things through knowing their inner essences, through direct participation in the divine ideas or divine energies that bring them into being—ideas and energies that are completely inaccessible to the perception of the reason. In a way that is again completely inaccessible to the reason, the spiritual intellect is capable of an immediate intuition and experience of the inner, eternal and absolute nature of everything that is. Its way of knowing is through spiritual experience and intuition and not through concepts and discursive reasoning. As St Maximos the Confessor puts it: 'The immediate experience of a thing suppresses the concept which represents this thing. I call experience knowledge in act which takes place beyond all concept. I call intuition the participation itself in the object known at a level beyond that of (rational and logical) thought'.[12]

The corollory, then, to the idea that man is a creature who lives through participation in the divine is that inherent in his nature, though it may be only in a dormant state, is the power or faculty through which this participation may be affected: a power or faculty that is as it were a seed or germ implanted in him at birth, upon whose development depends his growth into the full stature of manhood. It is this power or faculty which above all constitutes the image of God in man—image here being understood with those connotations of kinship and affinity which in Platonic thought link and relate the image to its archetype. But, we said, Christian theologians are careful not to identify this spiritual subject too exclusively with man's sole reality, because such identification would seem to imply a purely negative attitude to the reality of his soul and body. On the model of the hypostatic union of the divine and the human in Christ, they affirm on the contrary that soul and body are also susceptible to that process of *perichoresis*—that penetration of the divine into the human and the human into the divine. They too are capable of participation in the divine and consequently are or may be aspects of the image of God in man. They are or may be an integral part of man's eternal nature.

Modern thought, with its distrust of anything that escapes rational analysis, has practically eliminated the word 'soul' from its vocabulary—an elimination not unrelated of course to the chronic sterility or bankruptcy of this thought in the face of what is the first concern of any philosophical speculation worthy of the name: the question of our living identity. The Christian authors, however, on whom I draw for the substance of this chapter were more wholly engaged in the pursuit of our living identity than we tend to be. For them the soul is that highly charged complex of thought, feeling and sensitivity with which God endows us at birth. It is all that in me by virtue of which I am conscious of myself, through which and by means of which I experience myself as a living reality, as an 'I am'. It is in fact the one reality about which I can have a sure and direct knowledge. About everything else I may have doubts; but I cannot—unless I am a lunatic—question the reality of my own soul, because simply to ask the question implies the existence of the questioner.

At the same time the word, soul, is an ambiguous term. It is ambiguous first because it may be used with the sense that it includes the spiritual intellect, the eye of the soul, or with the sense that it is distinguished from the spiritual intellect. Second, it is ambiguous because, although created immortal and filled with divine light, it can nevertheless turn away from the light and be filled with darkness. Like the spiritual intellect itself, it stands between angel and devil. Being subject to persuasion and distracted by its likes and dislikes, it can be led away from its own centre and dominated by extraneous influences. It may even assert itself to such an extent that it has the Satanic conviction of its own independence and so denies the real source of its being: the assertion of the independence of the reason over the last few centuries—the *cogito ergo sum*—is an example of such Satanic possession of the soul.

This assertion of independence is, as I have already remarked, a clear sympton of what we call the Fall; and in these circumstances the soul, identified now with the selfhood, can be our own worst enemy, that self which is to be 'denied'[13] and which all—all, that is to say, who would be true disciples—must 'hate',[14] and which must be 'lost'[15] as a condition of regeneration. Indeed, it is the freeing or purifying of the soul from extraneous influences so that it may again be integrated with its inner source that is the purpose of so much ascetic and contemplative practice. In this respect it might be said that the function of the power or faculty of the spiritual intellect in virtue of which above all we may be said to be made in the image of God and upon whose 'awakening' in us depends our whole capacity for growth, is to mediate between the divine and our soul, bringing it ever more under the influence of the transfiguring light of the Spirit, carrying it, as it has been expressed, into the Godhead.

Yet it is not the soul alone that is brought under the influence of this transfiguring light and carried into the Godhead. Through the soul, the body also shares in this regeneration. For although the body comes into existence from the underlying matter of the world—from the earth—and so is an element in some ways independent of the soul, with its own form of consciousness, none the less there is an indissoluble relationship between soul and body. The soul is never bodiless and the body can never be without the soul. The soul and body of each single person are united together from the beginning of their existence, and the principle of this union lies in God

Himself: my identity as a creature with soul and body pre-exists in the dynamic and creative will and energy of God; and it is by virtue of this same creative will and energy that my soul and body have their indissoluble co-existence. Without each other—if that were possible—neither soul nor body could be complete. They complete each other; they mutually determine each other.

Moreover, when this union is said to be indissoluble, it is not simply within the context of this mortal life that this is meant. It is indissoluble after what we call death. There is no resurrection of the soul without that of the body, no resurrection of the body without that of the soul. Soul penetrates into body and body into soul, and this interchange, this transmigration of the one into the other, is a process that has no end. So intimate and reciprocal is this relationship that, as the divine and the human in Christ, so the soul and body in man are permanently united. With the spiritual intellect, they form a single composite nature, a single person or hypostasis, though fully to understand the significance of this may mean that we have to modify what tend to be our ideas about the nature of the body.

I will explain briefly what is implied in this. We have become so used to viewing things in accordance with our single vision of the material world that we automatically identify our body solely with its solid material elements, its outward form. This, for us, constitutes our body. It also represents a singularly truncated way of looking at things. Indeed, unless one is to disregard many of the central experiences recorded not only in scripture but also in the lives of many saints and holy men and women, one has to recognize that the body formed of gross material elements is really a kind of condensation or husk or outer wrapping of a body of a far more subtle texture; and that within the outer material body, and interpenetrating it, is an organism of a finer kind of matter, of a finer and more fluid kind of substance. In fact, the whole of what we call the solid universe is but a hardened or crystallized form of this finer kind of matter, a spiritual energy frozen and arrested; and to this our physical body is no exception.

Many early Christian writers have given intimations of what is here being said.[16] St Paul, for instance, in the fifteenth chapter of the first Epistle to the Corinthians, speaks of the resurrection in terms of the difference between the natural and the spiritual body. The body of flesh which is laid in the tomb is the natural body; the body that rises again is the spiritual body. St Paul illustrates this from the natural world: a grain of corn, he says, is sown in the ground as the natural body is laid in the grave. From the grain the plant grows, just as from the natural body the spiritual body will also grow. This of course implies that the spiritual body is from the first present in the natural body in a dormant and undeveloped state, just as the germ from which the plant will grow is concealed within the husk of the grain.

St Paul elaborates on this in the fifth chapter of the second Epistle to the Corinthians. There he contrasts the spiritual dwelling prepared for him in heaven with the material or fleshly dwelling he possesses on this earth. The argument seems largely to turn on the fact that death apparently strips us of our earthly body while the resurrection clothes us in a more glorious body. After death we do not possess a material body of flesh—'flesh and blood cannot inherit the kingdon of heaven'—but we will possess a new spiritual garment. We will be out of the flesh, but in a spiritual body. From this it is clear that St Paul distinguishes between the material body and the spiritual body, and regards the spiritual body as existing within us now in a germ-like state. The material body will be destroyed; but the spiritual body will be raised up and is already now within the material body, permeating it and acting through it in one way or another.

The kind of understanding that St Paul formulates is found also in the writings of many Christian saints. St Makarios of Egypt,[17] for example, appears to regard the soul, and even perhaps the spirit, as composed of a fine and subtle substance. He seems to maintain that a spiritual being does not merely possess a spiritual body but actually is such a body. As our flesh is organized out of the material stuff which forms the external world, so our spirits are formed out of the spiritual stuff or spiritual matter composing the invisible world in which they live. 'For every creature', he writes, 'is in its proper nature a body, whether angel, soul or devil. For though they are of fine texture, nevertheless in their fabric, quality and form, they are, in the fineness of their nature, bodies of fine texture, just as this outward body is in its fabric gross.'

This passage by St Makarios, and others like it, indicate a distinction that goes beyond the Pauline distinction between the material body and the spiritual body. They indicate that there is a kind of intermediate state between the material and the spiritual. In addition to the material earthly body and the spiritual body there is also an intermediate body, more subtle than the earthly body but not so glorious or splendid or fine as the spiritual body. This intermediate body might well be called the soul-body. In other words, man possesses, in various degrees of actualization, bodily forms that are spiritual, psychic and material, together with all the various interconnecting forms that link these levels one with another. He thus epitomizes in his own being the whole Platonic hierarchy of forms, or images, stretching from heaven to earth, of which we have already spoken. As a threefold composite of spirit, soul and body, he touches, when he is fully developed on all worlds, all levels of being, and includes them all within his span.

Indeed, it is this threefold character of man—the fact that through his spiritual intellect, which is so much more than merely rational, he has an affinity with the divine, while with his body he is linked to the material world—that gives him such a key position and role in the universe. He stands between God and the material world, between heaven and earth. In the old formula, he is the microcosm.[18] In fact, all things in creation have their meeting-place in man, and man is potentially all things. Properly seen, nothing is external to him. This is in contradistinction to the modern scientific view of things, which presupposes precisely that man does regard the world of nature as an object external to himself. It presupposes a loss of that consciousness in which nature is seen as part of his own subjectivity, as the living garment of his own inner being. Consequently man has also lost the sense of his role in relationship to the rest of creation. Displacing himself from nature, depersonalizing and objectifying it, he has destroyed the harmony and reciprocity that should exist between them.

The mechanistic character of modern science is marked by a desire to dominate, to master and possess and to exploit nature, not to transform it, or to hallow it. It presumes that the earth belongs to man, not man to the earth. In this it simply reflects the self-assertion of its agent, the disinherited reason which, having completed its revolt against what surpasses it, now seeks to impose its laws over the rest of life. Man's loss of his sense of harmony and reciprocity with nature—his destruction of the nuptial bonds between them— is itself the consequence of his loss of his sense of his status and role as the link between heaven and earth, the channel through which all commerce between them passes.

For man is called upon to mediate between heaven and earth, between God and His creation. But when he closes his consciousness to what is above it, he obstructs that flow through which material things may be saturated by the Spirit or the Spirit may become incarnate, and the result is a disorder in creation which brutalizes both man and nature. Because it is only through man fulfilling his role as mediator between God and the world that the world itself can fulfil its destiny and be transfigured in the light and presence of God. It is in this sense that man—when he is truly human—is also and above all a priest—the priest of God: he who offers the world to God in his praise and worship and who simultaneously bestows divine love and beauty upon the world.

In this respect, man is more than simply the microcosm, the homologous reflection of the created universe in which he participates. He is also the macrocosm. For—and it is this which has been perhaps the central theme of this chapter—in the end it is the divine Logos Himself who is the true ground, the true and ultimate subject of human nature; and it is only through man's realization of this—through his so bringing himself to the fulness of his being that God becomes the creative centre of his own personal and subjective life—that he achieves his true humanity and does justice to the cosmic implications of Christ's work of reconciliation. It is in Christ that the wall of separation between heaven and earth, the supernatural and the natural, the sacred and the profane is destroyed in the living sacrament of the divine love and presence. God's enhumanization has not only 'taken manhood into God'; it has also taken the whole created world into God, has resurrected it and transfigured it in its very depths.

It is only man's continuing alienation from the ground of his being that prevents him from realizing this, that throws a veil of opacity between God and man, God and the world, and keeps them in a state of false division and disunity. Correspondingly, it is through overcoming this alienation, and through remaking himself in the image and likeness of the divine that is at the heart of his own subjective life and that confers on him his unique quality as a person, that he shares in the priesthood of Christ and in that sacrament of love and beauty in which all things, released from their bondage, live, move and have their being. Outside this relationship, apart from this sacrament, man has no real place in the world, or the world in him. He is but a tormented shadow of himself, and his world a forsaken wilderness, and on both he is compelled to seek ever further revenge for that crime against his own nature which he refuses to acknowledge, still more to expiate.

2

Christian Theology and the Eclipse of Man

AT THE CONCLUSION of the last chapter I spoke of man as being above all a priest, the priest of God. I might equally well have said that he is above all an artist. He is an artist in that he is created in the image of the divine artist, which means that he is a work of art because he is that image and an artist because of his ability to imitate the Creator in producing 'works' after the pattern of the divine. Indeed, it is as artist that man most completely fulfils his function as mediator: for the function of art, properly understood, is to reveal to things the beauty hidden within them, to reveal to things their essential being and identity.

In this sense, man's great work of art is the perfecting of himself, for as man is an artist he has also the task of revealing to himself what he truly is, of perfecting his own shape. One catches here an echo of the ancient maxim to the effect that though God made us without our co-operation, He cannot save us without our co-operation. One catches too an echo of the teaching that the final perfection of man is the vision of himself as he is in God.

It is from the point of view of this understanding of the purpose of art—and from this point of view alone—that it can be said that the more a man functions as an artist and the more the artist in man determines his whole activity, the more human he is. Again, it is from this point of view that one can see how essential the doctrine of the Incarnation is to any Christian understanding of man. For the Incarnation presupposes the ontological link uniting everything with its eternal archetype and at the same time it safeguards that link. In this respect, the union of the divine and the human in Christ is the model of all sacred art. Above all, it is the model of that work of art which is central to the Christian tradition, the Eucharist—the image of the Incarnation and that work in which man's function as mediator is also fulfilled because it is in and through the Eucharist that the cosmic implications of Christ's work of re-conciliation are re-evoked and energized.

This is why the gradual erosion of the significance of the Incarnation over the last centuries (to the point to which the whole idea of it appears to some to be virtually superfluous where Christian doctrine is concerned) has meant the erosion of the true significance of man as artist. Man has lost his sense of his role as mediator between God and the world; he has lost his sense that the forms of his art should mirror the divine and that unless his work possesses this sacramental quality it will be as vacuous and ugly as most of the articles which now surround our daily lives, public and private. A social order which deprives man and his practices of their sacramental quality is already dead, no matter what frenetic activity it may appear to manifest.

For what we have experienced over the last few centuries of our history is precisely a process whereby this understanding of man as priest and artist has been overlaid and even replaced by another conception of man. This process may be called an eclipse of man in that what it represents is the gradual obliteration of the idea that man is divinely-human, or is fully human only in so far as he is divine, and the substitution for it of the idea that man is human, and is or can be a person, simply in his own right, apart from God. What has been lost, that is to say, is the sense that there is a great discrepancy between man in his ordinary merely exterior self and man as a true being; and that what is essential in man, his deepest self, through which alone he is capable of developing into a true being, is the divine in him, this principle which is beyond him and outside him, belonging to another level of reality, and yet at the same time is the most subjective aspect of his own nature.

Modern man's chief heresy about himself consists in the fact that he thinks he is or can be man without any inner dynamic relationship with God, without that reciprocity and inter-penetration of the divine and the human of which the model is the incarnate Logos. He has more or less eliminated the idea of God-manhood from his mind. Having rejected the understand-ing that his life and activity are significant only in so far as they incarnate, reflect and radiate that transcendent spiritual reality which is the ground and centre of his own being, he is con-demned to believe that he is the autocratic and omnipotent ruler of his own affairs and of the world about him, which it is his right and duty to subdue, organize, investigate and exploit to serve his profane mental curiosity or his acquisitive material appetites. The deification of man as a fallen mortal entity has led, as we are only too well aware, to the most extreme forms of cruelty and rapacity, forms which deny the unique and absolute value of the human person and of every other created reality. The assertion that man is merely human has resulted in a dehumanization possibly without parallel in the history of the world.

The later stages of this process of dehumanization are the theme of the next chapter. In this chapter our task is to trace the developments, largely intellectual, which prepared the ground for these later stages. It is easy to see that the various notions about man that stem from the non-religious scientific humanism of the last few centuries are radically at odds with the Christian understanding of man outlined in the last chapter. But this non-religious scientific humanism grew in the first place out of the Christian matrix. It captured the European mind after that mind had been exposed to the teachings of Christianity for more than a thousand years. The implications of this would seem to be that the roots of this scientific human-ism must lie somewhere within Christianity itself.

There must have been certain developments within the intel-lectual world of Christendom which prepared the way for the rejection of its own doctrines. It is important to try to discern what these developments may have been and where they arose. At least it is important to do this if Christianity is to claim to have any creative intellectual role in the contemporary world. If Christianity is not to have any creative intellectual role, then the exercise is merely an academic one. But if it is, then those developments or inadequacies in its own tradition which prepared the ground for its own negation must be understood and counteracted. It is useless for Christians to try to grapple with and find solutions for contemporary problems if the only intellectual weapons they have to hand are those which contributed to the production of these problems in the first place.

What, then, faces us is the task of throwing light on the question of where, when and how the idea of God-manhood in its full radiance was obscured or displaced within the Christian theological tradition itself, a process which allowed tendencies hostile to Christianity to manifest themselves virtually in a Christian guise. The actual area of our investigation may be limited to the world of western Christianity. This is not only because the non-Christian developments with which we are concerned grew out of this world. It is also because the idea of God-manhood in the form in which I have expressed it remains the bedrock of the Orthodox Christian tradition down to the present day, however little it may be realized in practice.

Once again, it is with reference to Christology that we can best begin this enquiry. It should have been clear from the last chapter that what is meant by hypostasis in the Christian language is not merely a substance with its qualities in the Aristotelian sense, but a single and unique person. The hypostasis of Christ is such a person: a divine-human synthesis whose subject is the Logos of God. From the philosophical point of view, this understanding of Christ's person depends upon the recognition that as a substance in His own right—as a hypostasis, that is to say—He consists of two independent substances, the divine and human; and that it is through the interpenetration of these two substances, each preserving its own identity 'without division or confusion', that the unity of the two natures in Christ is constituted.

This is to say that, on the philosophical plane, behind the conception of the person of Christ as formulated in the great Christological discussions among the Greek Fathers, lies what is basically a Platonic understanding of the relationship between universal and particular, with its focus on the idea of the participation of the one in the other. I do not want to say by this that the Greek Fathers are Platonists and nothing more. This is to over-simplify. But I do want to say that in formulating their Christological conceptions they tacitly assume the kind of possibility visualized by Plato in his doctrine about substances, namely, that they are constituted through the mutual participation of one form in another, of one substance in another.

This means that in the Platonic perspective it is perfectly possible to envisage a substance—which is a unity—as consisting of more than one substance actually present in it. It is possible to envisage the unity of composite substances. And it is precisely in accordance with this possibility—this philosophical possibility—that the Greek Fathers formulated their conception of the person of Christ, or the substance of Christ, as a unity consisting of what amounts to two independent substances, the divine and the human.

This was the philosophical basis of their Christological ideas, and by extension this was the basis of their doctrine of man's deification, the doctrine of the God-man: a deification realized through the participation of the human element in the divine element without any loss of identity or integrity in either direction. The human image, that is to say, participates in the divine and universal archetype in the manner in which, in Platonic thought, particulars participate in their universal 'models', the divine ideas.

This understanding of the hypostasis of Christ in its turn provided, as we saw, the model according to which the relationship between soul and body in the human composite was envisaged. The two substances of soul and body are united in man, and both are actually present in him. Soul does not absorb body, or body soul. They co-exist, distinct but undivided; and the principle of their union lies in God Himself. Once again, the key to the understanding of both the relationship of soul to body in the single human being, and the relationship of the human being to the divine principle that consummates this union of soul and body in him, is to be found in the idea of participation which lies at the heart of Platonic doctrine.

These Christological and anthropological ideas, formulated

according to a philosophical ground-plan largely Platonic in character, are the corner-stones of the Greek patristic tradition. But they are also effective, broadly speaking, for the mediaeval western Christian tradition, to which our enquiry is now to be confined. I say 'broadly speaking' first because they were never formulated in the West with such clarity or completeness and second because their full significance was from the start vitiated by St Augustine's teaching on sin and free will which became so inextricably intertwined with the western Christian tradition.

Yet when due allowance is made for these limitations—and they are of great importance—it none the less remains true that, broadly speaking, from St Augustine himself down to the twelfth century Cistercian and Victorine writers, the western Christian understanding of man presupposes that same Platonic ground-plan which underlies the Greek patristic understanding. For them, too, a single substance may be composed of more than one form-giving substance actually present in it. Again, man is a case in point, for in man the two independent substances of soul and body are united and both remain actually present in him within this union.

Moreover—although St Augustine himself as a dogmatic theologian was formally to deny this possibility in the degree to which it is affirmed by the Greek Fathers[19]—the western contemplative tradition, like its eastern counterpart, tacitly or explicitly envisages that process of *perichoresis* through which the divine may become the actually present substance of human nature without on that account eliminating the substantial reality of soul and body. In other words, this tradition envisages the soul as including that supra-rational faculty or organ or power through which man may have a direct experience of the divine and through which the divine may penetrate into the human. But though the tendency throughout was to exalt the soul at the expense of the body, at least neither St Augustine nor the Platonists of the twelfth century had any intention of denying that soul and body are two independent substances actually present in their union in the single substance of man. St Augustine defines a man as a soul using a body, or as a soul possessing a body, but he adds that a soul possessing a body does not constitute two persons, but a single man;[20] and elsewhere he says: 'Man is a rational substance composed of a soul and a body, and there is no doubt that man has a soul which is not his body, and a body which is not his soul.'[21]

Similarly, by writers like William St-Thierry the soul might be regarded as virtually the whole man and the body as the least important part; but there is the same insistence on the unity of man and of soul and body in man. For this whole tradition, Platonic concepts served as a means of expressing the superiority of the soul over the body, but not of excluding the body from the unity of human nature. Yet basically this unity was not something that had to be verified or explained in philosophical terms; it was something that had to be verified through prayer and contemplation, through recognizing one's dignity as the image of God and through realizing it by opening the heart to the liberating love of God and by constant invocation of Him. It was above all on the basis of their experience that Christian thinkers from St Augustine to the contemplatives of the twelfth century affirmed man as a person in the union of soul and body regarded as two distinct but undivided entities.

If in general terms it is true to say that down to the twelfth century theology was regarded as the expression of a given reality which had to be confirmed in actual personal experience before it could be formulated in conformity with certain philosophical standards, in the twelfth century itself, and still more in the thirteenth and subsequent centuries, this ceased to be the case. In these centuries, the relationship between theology and experience in the West underwent a profound change. It was not so much that theology ceased to be regarded as the expression of a given reality—a reality given in revelation—as that now it was demanded that this expression should conform to certain philosophical standards quite apart from whether or not it was confirmed in actual personal experience.

Moreover, these philosophical standards were now those of Aristotle. Aristotle was translated into Latin from the beginning of the twelfth century, and by the end of the thirteenth century the old theological way of looking at the world, and at man in the world, had largely been replaced by a philosophical way that represented an attempt to adapt theology to the technical language of Aristotle. The extent to which this process of forcing Christian theology into the philosophical framework of Aristotelian principles involved a crippling of this theology at its heart has never been fully explored.[22] This may be chiefly due to the fact that those who might otherwise have been qualified to undertake such an exploration have themselves been committed to regarding this very process as a positive development of Christian theology and not as disastrous for it. Be that as it may, what can be said is that no branch of this theology—Christology, Eucharistic doctrine, anthropology—was left unaffected. The thirteenth century marks a new age within the Christian world. During it the Platonic elements which had served the earlier theologians as a vehicle for expressing an understanding of man confirmed through a life of prayer and contemplation were replaced by or codified in accordance with Aristotelian categories of a purely abstract and theoretical nature. European thought entered what might be called the epoch of abstraction, from which it has not yet emerged.

What effect did this Aristotelian revolution have on the theme with which we are directly concerned, the theme of man? Here again the danger is one of over-simplification. But I think the clue to the answer to this question has already been indicated. We have said that the Christological and anthropological ideas of the Greek Fathers, and by and large of western theologians down to the twelfth century, depended upon the acceptance of certain conceptual possibilities which may be described as Platonic. These possibilities in their turn presuppose what is basically a Platonic understanding of the relationship between the universal and the particular, the particular being the likeness or image of the universal which acts as its model and in whose invisible reality it participates through its inherence in the universal and its affinity with it.

It was on the basis of this understanding that Plato was able to formulate his conception of substances and essences which are really a network of participations, intelligible and ordered, constituting a hierarchical system of forms: the famous golden chain; and it was also on the basis of this understanding that Christian theologians were able to formulate their conception of the union of the two natures in Christ, the divine and the human, as the mutual inherence of two distinct substances constituting a unique person, or hypostasis, and their derivative conception of the union of soul and body in man as established in a similar manner. Moreover, it was on the possibility of the participation of the human in the divine without the loss of the identity or integrity of either element that these theologians were able to envisage the process of human deification on the model of the union of the two natures in Christ—a deification which presupposes an affinity and likeness between man and God, the image and the archetype.

It was precisely the kind of possibility affirmed in Platonic doctrine and assumed by the Greek Fathers that Aristotle's teachings denied. There is no need here to rehearse in detail the doctrinal differences and conflicts between Plato and Aristotle. It is enough to mention two inter-related points, the one negative and the other positive. First, Aristotle attacked and rejected the whole idea of universals as conceived by Plato, as well as its corollary, the idea of participation, either of substance in substance or of particular in the universal. For Aristotle,[23] a universal was merely an abstract class name, not an *idea* in the Platonic sense, that is to say, an identification of essence and existence; and on this basis he argued that no universal exists apart from concrete particulars and that no universal is a substance. It is impossible for a universal to be a substance because, according to Aristotle, the substance of each thing is peculiar to that thing, whereas the Platonic universal is by definition what can be present in a multiplicity of things.

For Aristotle, to say that universals, or the divine *ideas*, are models and that they can inhere in other things or that other things can participate in them is meaningless metaphor. There is, he asserts, no separate world of universals, and universals have existence only in so far as they characterize individual concrete things. It is this separateness and self-contained, or self-enclosed, nature of concrete things—of particulars—which typifies Aristotle's world, in contrast to the Platonic world in which the apparent separateness of particulars is not separateness at all but an inherence or participation in a medium in which the invisible reality of the universals is reflected and diffused.

Second, as the positive aspect of his criticism of the Platonic doctrine of universals, Aristotle puts forward his own idea of substance.[24] Here we approach what is crucial for the understanding of later developments. A substance in the Aristotelian sense—and we are speaking of what Aristotle calls primary substances—is the originative source and cause of a thing, that which makes a thing what it is and nothing else, and gives it its unity. It is not another element in the thing alongside of its material elements, or anything compounded out of elements. It is the whole thing, including the qualities and attributes implicit in it. It implies qualities, but these are not something outside it which it needs in addition to itself; and though it is prior to qualities it cannot exist without them, just as they cannot exist without it. A qualityless substance is as impossible as a quality which does not presuppose a substance.

As the whole thing, substance has a separate existence in the manner of particular entities. It belongs only to itself and to that which possesses it. It cannot consequently be present in a multiplicity of particulars simultaneously, and so it cannot be a universal in the Platonic sense. Substances for Aristotle cannot be shared or participated. Every substance in the universe is absolutely individual; indeed, this primacy of individual substance is one of the cardinal points of Aristotle's thought, the point about which he most clearly differs from Plato.

It follows that, as an individual unit, a substance cannot consist of other substances. Substances cannot mingle or interpenetrate and there can be no composite substances such as one can envisage according to Platonic thought. That is to say, a substance cannot consist of other substances actually present in it: two cannot come to be from one, or one from two. For a thing to have one substance is *ipso facto* for it to be deprived of any other substance. The destruction of one substance is the generation of another, and *vice versa*: two substances cannot co-exist in the same entity.

In the light of what we have said about the Platonic assumptions underlying the formulation of Christian doctrine, Christological and anthropological, it should not be difficult to see how the application to it of these Aristotelian standards could not but have a devastating effect. First, where Christology is concerned, the application of Aristotle's teaching on substance, as outlined above, meant that the union of the divine and the human natures in Christ could no longer be conceived as the union of two substances, each preserving its own integral identity in and through the union: the whole idea of the *perichoresis* as envisaged by the Greek Fathers was precluded, as also was the idea that Christ can be the ultimate ground or subject of each single person, who is thereby 'deified'. The Incarnation could be envisaged as something that occurred only in the unique case of the historical figure of Jesus, and not also as something that involves human nature as a whole and so something in which every individual participates. The idea of Christ as a universal in the Platonic sense was now more or less meaningless, and so for the same reason was the whole ancient doctrine of the universal and divine Logos, according to which the divine can be actually present in all things without those things on that account losing their own substantial identity.

Moreover, this drastic restriction in scope of the significance of the Incarnation was reflected in an equally truncated doctrine of the Eucharist: since a single entity must be defined by a single substance and no two substances can be in the same entity at the same time, the only way in which it was possible to explain the 'real presence' in the eucharistic elements was to say that through consecration the elements are 'transubstantiated'. That is to say, through consecration the substance of the bread and wine is destroyed and is replaced by the substance of Christ's Body and Blood. In fact, because of this same restriction of the Incarnation to the unique case of the historical figure of Jesus and the corresponding inability to envisage the Logos as a universal in the Platonic sense, the 'real presence' itself in the Eucharist could be accounted for only by formulating the grotesque notion that Christ is actually sacrificed afresh and actually dies afresh at each Eucharist.

It is, however, in connection with the understanding of man proposed by St Thomas Aquinas that the effect of the application of Aristotelian standards may be seen in the way that is most relevant in this context.[25] It should be said at once that the Thomistic conception of man is not Aristotelian. Rather it was St Thomas' intention to maintain the traditional Christian understanding of man as expressed by, for instance, St.Augustine, but to strip this expression of its Platonic elements and to reframe it in accordance with the technical language of Aristotle. It is not a question of doubting the probity of St Thomas' intention or belittling his achievement. But having said that, it yet remains true that the effect of St Thomas' attempt to place this understanding within the Aristotelian framework was to buckle it in such a way that to all intents and purposes it was radically altered.

As I said in the last chapter, when speaking of the Christian understanding of man, the crux of this understanding is the recognition that man's sovereign faculty or organ of knowing is not the reason and that his knowledge is not consequently confined to the sphere of the rational. He possesses in addition to the reason a supra-rational faculty or organ, one through which he is capable of entering into direct communion with the divine, of experiencing directly spiritual or metaphysical realities, and so of knowing the truth or nature of each thing, including himself, by knowing the creative but uncreated idea or type or energy of which it, or he, is the expression. He may know things, including himself, by knowing how they are in God. He is not, that is to say, simply a twofold being, of soul and body, but he is a threefold being, of whom the third component—this supra-rational, more-than-human faculty—is as it were the spiritual subject, a seed or germ of spiritual awareness dwelling in the soul and illuminating the soul while not being identified with it.

I said further that it is through the development of this faculty—a development which corresponds to bringing it from a passive or latent to an active or conscious state within him and which is the purpose of the ascetic and other practices of the contemplative tradition—that man grows into the fullness of his nature. He becomes a deified being, a God-man. Without this recognition—without the recognition that God can be the substance of our human nature without the substance of this nature being on that account replaced or destroyed—the whole theory on which the contemplative tradition is based, and the whole doctrine of deification which is part of that tradition, fall to the ground and become to all intents and purposes meaningless.

Yet it is precisely this recognition—and here we are at the heart of that radical shift in Christian understanding from which so much stems—which for St Thomas is precluded because of his adherence to Aristotelian principles. For St Thomas, God cannot Himself be directly present in man, in such a way that He is the active subject of man's being, because He—God—being a substance in His own right, cannot be present in another substance, man, without displacing or destroying it. Consequently, He can be present to man but indirectly, as a created light: God illumines man by creating him with an agent intellect, but He cannot Himself be the intellectual agent of the human soul.[26]

For St Thomas, man is certainly in a position to know things, including himself, in a limited manner, and he is also in a position to understand the relationship between things and his own concepts about them. In other words, in addition to his sensory perception of things, man can know them through rational judgement and reflection. But it is very different where the relationship between things, including man himself, and the creative mind of God is concerned.

This relationship between things and their archetypal ideas or energies in God—a knowledge of which alone would give us a true knowledge of things, including ourselves, because it is in it and through it that the truth and identity of things primarily and properly exists—cannot, according to St Thomas, be formally known by us. We can know things, including ourselves, only externally, and not in their inner truth and identity. We can know the copy, but not the relation this copy has to the archetype, not the correspondence between what has been created and the Creator. According to St Thomas, we have no power or faculty or organ of intelligence through which we can perceive and know this correspondence.[27]

This is to say that in the Thomistic view man is not a threefold but a twofold being. He is no more than a soul-body composite and of these two elements the soul is by definition the rational soul, and its knowledge is a purely rational knowledge. Moreover, lacking any faculty through which he can know and experience things, including himself, as they are in

God, man is forced to depend for his knowledge, including what he calls his spiritual knowledge, on sense perception. 'Although through Revelation we can become capable of knowing things which we otherwise would not know,' St Thomas writes, 'we do not know them in any other way than through the senses.'[28] And this knowledge itself, which has its starting point in, and must always remain somehow dependent upon, sense perception, is and must be restricted to the sphere of the rational. It would seem that the declension from Christian doctrine usually associated above all with the rationalist philosophers of the last few centuries was already foreshadowed in the thought of St Thomas Aquinas.

If we are to ask why this radical shift and re-orientation of Christian understanding was forced on St Thomas by his subscription to Aristotelian principles, the answer, I think, is again connected with Aristotle's teaching on substance about which I have been speaking. St Thomas accepted this teaching on the unity of the substantial form. It was therefore impossible for him to admit that the divine can be the indwelling subject of each single individual human being, and so the indwelling principle of the unity of his soul and body, because according to this teaching which he accepted it is impossible to envisage a substance consisting of more than one substance actually present in it. Hence it would be impossible for the divine to be the substance of the human person without the destruction of the human substance itself.

This means that man is now projected outside the subjective ground of his being, outside that point in himself at which he is able to integrate soul and body subjectively through a penetration into the spiritual principle of this integration. The mystery of the unity of soul and body in man can be grasped, not merely on the level of mental ideas but existentially, only through participation in that divine will and energy which are the principle of this unity. It is by becoming conscious of the divine Logos as the ultimate subjective ground of his being that man can grasp the unity of the duality of his nature. Outside this ground he can but grasp this unity on the abstract mental plane. He becomes merely the object of his own thought, not the integrator of his nature.

It is to this that man condemns himself when he fails to take into account the more-than-human element in himself through whose dynamic realization alone he can achieve his dignity as a divine-human person, a God-man. He no longer seeks to realize this element because he no longer regards it as a possibility inherent in his nature; and if you do not envisage the possibility of something—or, rather, if your conceptual framework excludes a certain possibility—then you are not likely to set about trying to realize it with any great enthusiasm. Instead, man is now forced to regard himself as consisting solely of the two 'objective' and created elements of soul and body, brought and held together by another object, external to himself, which is God.

The whole basis of the ascetic and contemplative tradition of Christianity, whose purpose is the transfiguration of man through his penetration into the divine and God's penetration into man—the birth of God in man which is simultaneously the birth of man in God—is in this way radically undermined; and the theology of its exponents, confirmed in their own experience, is replaced by arguments which presuppose that the ontological realities to which they refer conform to the principles of Aristotelian logic. We have entered the world not only of abstraction but also of objectivization. In other terms, we have entered the world which we in our vanity describe as characterized by the death of God but which is far more accurately described as characterized by the death of man.

When we turn to the Thomistic understanding of the actual relationship between soul and body in man further effects of the application of these Aristotelian principles at once become evident. The traditional view of this relationship is, as we have seen, that soul and body constitute two distinct substances brought together through the creative will and energy of God. This relationship, once established, is indissoluble; and so intimate and reciprocal is it that soul and body together have one common substance, one common hypostasis, which is precisely the divine will and energy that have brought them into union. Through this participation in the divine, soul and body are integral to man's eternal nature. They are susceptible to that process of deification which consists in the ever deepening penetration of the human into the divine, of the divine into the human; and throughout this process the body, although under the transfiguring influence of the Spirit it may grow increasingly more subtle and transparent, does not cease to keep its distinct identity. The body too, as an integral part of human nature, shares in the resurrection.

This view of the relationship between soul and body as the union of two distinct substances was again precluded for St Thomas by his acceptance of the Aristotelian proposition that a substance, which is a unity, cannot consist of more than one substance actually present in it. Moreover, in accordance with this same proposition, which excludes the idea of the participation of one substance in another, he could not envisage, as we noted, the divine Logos Himself as the indwelling principle of the soul-body union in man. He was therefore compelled to identify both the unique substance of man and the indwelling principle of his unity as a composite being with some other principle. In effect, he identified them with the soul. For St Thomas, the human soul is the unique substantial form of man and the principle of man's unity as a soul-body composite.

In affirming this, however, St Thomas encountered a certain difficulty. In strict Aristotelian terms the form of a material entity is itself material and so corruptible. Thus, if the soul, on the lines of the Aristotelian form, has existence only through the composite whose substantial form it is, then as the form of matter it would be no more immaterial and no more immortal than matter itself. Hence, if the soul is the substantial form of the body it too must be material, corruptible and mortal. But if the soul is material and corruptible and mortal, then immortality is impossible for man, since he does not and cannot, according to St Thomas, contain in himself any more-than-human element, any divine seed through whose realization he can achieve his immortality. Hence, in strict Aristotelian terms, if the soul is the form of the body, man is but a creature doomed to extinction at the end of his mortal life, a prospect of which the whole Christian message is a denial. In order therefore to safeguard the possibility of man's immortality while at the same time remaining loyal to those Aristotelian principles to which Christian doctrine was now being submitted, St Thomas was compelled to take a further step and to affirm that the soul itself is by definition a self-subsistent spiritual substance, one that receives the act of being in itself, and so is by nature immaterial, incorruptible and immortal.

In affirming this, however, St Thomas overcame one difficulty only to encounter another. In Aristotelian terms, a spiritual substance is something that subsists by and through itself. But a form is found only in something else. Hence, again in Aristotelian terms, a spiritual substance cannot be the substantial form of the body. Yet this is what St Thomas makes it. 'In the individual man,' he writes, 'there is no other substantial form than the rational soul, and. . . through the rational soul man is not only man, but also animal and living and body and substance and being.'[29] At this point therefore St Thomas violates strict Aristotelian principles. For him, a spiritual form—the soul—is both a substance within itself and the substantial form of a material body; and since as a spiritual substance the soul transcends that body with which it shares its spiritual existence, it preserves its immateriality, incorruptibility and immortality even though it is the substantial form of the body.

Yet in establishing the unity and integrity of man as a soul-body composite in this way, St Thomas is forced to deprive the body of any substantial reality in its own right. For St Thomas, soul and body constitute a single and unique essence because they are joined together as parts within a single existence. But as two substances cannot co-exist within a single entity, it is the soul alone which in St Thomas' scheme possesses any substantial reality. The single existence of the soul-body composite is in fact that of the soul. The body is what it is merely through the soul.

Moreover, as a spiritual substance, the soul transcends the body. Why, then, it might be asked, does it need a body at all? St Thomas' answer is that it needs a body because it—the soul—is endowed with certain intellectual and sensible powers which can be exercised only through the body. It cannot, in other words, fulfil its nature unless it is joined to a body. The soul needs a historical existence in a material body in order to express and to realize the powers proper to it. In a sense, it is incomplete unless it has a body, and the aptitude and inclination to inform a body are part and parcel of its nature.[30] This is the reason why man is a composite being: the human soul requires a body for its completion. But this compositeness is for the sake of the soul, not for the sake of the body. It is the soul which, although it transcends matter, needs a material body in order to perform its functions as a spiritual substance. The fact itself of human compositeness lies entirely within the spiritual substance of the soul.

It follows from this that although theoretically man for St Thomas is a soul-body composite, in actuality as a whole he can be explained only in the light of his soul. It is in the soul that his total reality as a man is prefigured. Though the soul is said to be part of man, ultimately man is no more than the soul in the fulness of its nature. It might be said that in the Thomistic view man is a function of the soul, not soul a function of man. At all events, whereas before St Thomas it was possible to think of the soul as the most important part of man, after St Thomas it was possible to think of man as complete without a body at all, because what the body contributes as an organic and material instrument is already present within the soul in a spiritual form and as a spiritual exigency.

For St Thomas man *qua* man (a soul-body composite) does not have a nature: he only has a history. Man is but an incident, a phase, in the history of his soul. Again theoretically, since man by definition is not a soul alone but a soul possessing a body, his beatitude must also be that of a composite; and hence the resurrection of the body is a philosophical demand and not simply a matter of faith. But the conclusion which St Thomas' thought suggests is that once the soul has expressed and realized that part of its intellectuality which can be expressed and realized only through man—that is to say, through the soul becoming incarnate and engaged in an incarnated and temporal life—then man's *raison d'être* as a soul-body composite will disappear and the soul will revert to its status of being merely a human soul, bodiless.

It is out of St Thomas' conception of man that rises that spectre of the bodiless soul which is so to bedevil theology in the post-scholastic age, engendering those endless debates on such topics as how many such souls can dance, booted and spurred, upon the point of a needle. It might even be said that St Thomas' attempts to preserve the understanding of the integrity of man while submitting the expression of this understanding to Aristotelian standards has resulted in a conception of man that cripples this integrity at its very heart by negating the value of the body as a substantial reality in its own right. In short, it may be said that the categories through which St Thomas tried to express Christian doctrine were such that they effectively obscured or even excluded the traditional Christian understanding of man.

The full consequences, however, of identifying the substantial reality of man to all intents and purposes with the soul and of regarding the soul as exclusively rational in its nature became apparent in the thought of the next major figure in this lineage, the figure of Descartes;[31] for it is in the thought of Descartes that the way prepared by St Thomas is consolidated in a radical dualism between soul and body, mind and matter, in which the body, along with the rest of the physical world, is regarded as totally deprived of all spiritual or non-material qualities and powers.

Descartes followed the Scholastics in his theory of the union of soul and body; that is to say, he conceived the soul as related to the body in the way in which, within the world of purely material bodies, forms are related to matter in Aristotelian thought; and following St Thomas he regarded the soul as the substantial form of the body. But while for St Thomas the soul is made to inform the body and can complete its nature as a substance only on condition that it does so inform the body, for Descartes the soul is a complete substance by definition, quite apart from the body.

Descartes defines substance as that which exists in such a way that it has no need of any other thing in order to exist; and something can be perceived to be a substance when we can conceive it as existing without any other thing. Since we can conceive of the soul as existing in this way—as existing, that is to say, apart from corporeal members—the soul is a substance. This means that the soul is complete in itself, without the body. It may be joined to the body, but it does not need the body in order to complete its nature. In fact, it is strictly opposed to the body. The soul is entirely a *res cogitans*, a *mens*. It is a substance whose whole nature or essence is rational thought. Ultimately, there are two types of reality: that of things that think and that of things that do not think. The soul—or the mind, for the two are synonymous for Descartes—belongs to the first type. To the second belong all materials things, including the body, and these are entirely without spiritual or psychic forces or qualities.

For Descartes, the distinction between the soul and body is real and absolute. Both are complete substances in themselves, and neither can possess the properties of the other: the soul cannot possess the properties of matter or the body the properties of thought. There can be no interpenetration between them, no process of *perichoresis*. Indeed, while in traditional Christian thought it is impossible to conceive the soul as existing without the body, or the body without the soul, in terms of Cartesian thought it is hard to conceive how the two can unite at all, so completely is the notion of the one purified of and distinguished from the notion of the other, the notion of the *res cogitans* from that of the *res extensa*.

The body itself is a machine, something like a watch or a hydraulic automaton. Physiology is a chapter of mechanics. Cartesian biology is experimental; but such experiments discover the structures and functions which can and must be conceived according to mechanical and soulless models, because basically nature itself is mechanical and soulless. Already in Descartes' thought is implicit, if not explicit, that concept of the plurality of distinct and non-participative substances each with its own specific properties which a century later was to issue in the notion that chemical change itself is but a purely mechanical process.

At all events, with Descartes the conceptual framework which has given birth to modern science is established. From this framework the idea of God-manhood, already so reduced by the schoolmen, is rigorously and relentlessly excluded. Man is now regarded as a more or less autonomous entity existing as it were apart from God. He is thought of as being nothing more than an individual and finite creature, and his reason, cut off and closed to all that is above it, is regarded as the sole instrument and arbiter of his knowledge, anything that transcends the reason being treated quite simply as non-knowledge or, which is the same thing, as the sub-product of a hallucinatory and irrelevant imagination.

As for this knowledge itself, it has nothing sacred about it. It does not refer to any sacred or qualitative reality, and it does not require from man any deep inner transformation and *ascesis* in order to acquire it: there is no awareness any longer of the bond that links knowledge of the truth and the state of purity so intimately that there can be no knowing in any but an abstract and impersonal sense until such purity is attained. On the contrary, what is now regarded as knowledge is something entirely profane and, in so far as it refers to anything at all, it refers but to a nature that is seen as dead, alien and purely functional and quantitative. As such, this knowledge is at the disposal of any deft investigator who will exert his brain but who at the same time may be mean-spirited, selfish, and given over to pursuits as self-corruptive as they are trivial. In other words, we have entered the world of modern science, with all its consequences for human and natural life.

3

Modern Science & the Dehumanization of Man

IN THE PREVIOUS chapter I have traced the intellectual developments that led to the emergence of the modern scientific outlook. In this chapter I will carry the analysis a stage further and show how the growing ascendancy of this outlook and its translation into social forms have gone hand in hand with a dehumanization of both man and society.

Such a process of dehumanization is not of course accidental. On the contrary, it is inevitable once the norms of the modern scientific outlook begin to be applied in the sphere of human and social relationships for the simple reason that, as I shall elucidate, an inhumanity is built into the very presuppositions on which this outlook is based. We have to remember that the 'clear' and 'distinct' notions that form the basis of modern science are not clear and distinct in and for themselves, but only in the context of a certain set of concepts and axioms. Men like Galileo and Descartes did not simply have to replace one set of theories by a better set. They had to destroy one world and replace it by another. They had to destroy one conceptual framework of the mind and replace it by another.

Modern science presupposes a radical reshaping of our whole mental outlook. It involves a new approach to being, a new approach to nature, in short, a new philosophy. Borne over the last few centuries on the wave of the excitement of formulating and applying this new philosophy, we have tended to take it for granted that it represents a great break-through, a marvellous advance on the part of mankind, even a sign of our coming of age. Now that we begin to see the consequences of our capitulation to it—and we are only now beginning to see these consequences—we are not so sure. But even so it is difficult for us to admit that, far from being an advance, the whole modern scientific experiment may be a ghastly failure. Yet there is no reason why it should not be. One has to judge things by their fruits. And one of the fruits of modern science, clear for all to see, and implicit in the philosophy on which it is based, is the dehumanization both of man and of the society that he has built in its name.

I have said that the scientific revolution of the seventeenth century could be consolidated only through the destruction of one order and its replacement by another. Briefly, in terms of western civilization, the order which modern science has replaced is that of the mediaeval Christian world. This Christian society was an organically integrated society. It was a kind of sacred order established by God in which everything, not only man and man's artifacts, but every living form of plant, bird or animal, the sun, moon and stars, the waters and the mountains, were seen as signs of things sacred (*signa rei sacrae*), expressions of a divine cosmology, symbols linking the visible and the invisible, earth and heaven. It was a society dedicated to ends which are ultimately supra-terrestrial, non-temporal, beyond the limits of this world.

Indeed, a great deal of effort in this Christian world went into preserving, fostering and nourishing the sense of realities that we now call supernatural. Throughout the length and breadth of this world visible images of these realities were set up and venerated, in icons, crosses, churches, shrines, in the collective ritual. They were the endless pursuit of monasteries, as of the saints and holy men who moved among the populace as naturally as birds among the leaves. Even when these saints and holy men retreated into solitude, everyone living in the world was aware that the woods and hills, the wildernesses and caves surrounding his home were peopled with these men ready to give counsel and benediction.

The highest type of activity in the mediaeval Christian world had nothing to do with what is practical or productive or efficient as we understand these terms. The highest type of activity was that of contemplation; and although the summits of this contemplative activity may have been reached by but a few, yet the realities among which this few lived were an undisputed and central fact of common awareness. At the same time, this awareness did not eclipse man's sense of his status as a creature of earth, shaped out of the earth and returning to it, his whole inner being nourished and enriched by his organic contact with nature and with the breath of the Spirit that had fashioned him as nature's masterwork. This mediaeval Christian world also of course had its injustices and cruelties, its deprivations and ugliness, its suffering and sickness. It is not a question of idealizing this world, of seeing it transfigured by our nostalgia, still less of proposing a return to it. It is one simply of indicating its overriding spiritual orientation and pursuits.

Here I would like to make a digression to dispel a common misunderstanding, one intimately related to our theme. It is often said, when this contrast between the mediaeval and the modern scientific world is made, that the mediaeval world also had its scientific techniques and that these were not developed because no one knew how to develop them. It is not quite so simple as this. It is true that the mediaeval world had its techniques. But these techniques deliberately were not employed or developed beyond a certain point—the point at which they would begin to impede or prevent what was far more important: the realization of the overriding imaginative view of life. Here the primary concern was religious, not technical, and technical processes that upset the overriding conceptions of harmony, beauty and balance were, quite simply, rejected.

This may seem strange to us today. We have become so used to the technical mastery of the West that we often go so far as to characterize the western mentality in general as practical and concrete, and to contrast it with the contemplative spirit of the East. In fact we even go further and see a direct lineal connection between the spirit of Christianity with its emphasis on the Incarnation and hence, it is supposed, on the reality of matter, and the emergence of the modern scientific mentality and its concomitants, the exploration and exploitation of nature; and we contrast this materialistic spirit of Christianity with the more transcendentally-minded spirit of Hinduism or Buddhism or even of Islam, for which matter tends to be regarded as a kind of illusion, lacking all subsistent reality.

This view is of course a gross over-simplification and in many ways is the reverse of the truth.[32] Until the modern period, it was the East that had the concrete 'experimental' mind, not the West, and it was the East and not the West that possessed the mastery of techniques and technical processes, whether these had material or magical purposes, or purposes directly connected with the realization of the spiritual life. The idea of 'method', whether applied to material or spiritual techniques, is above all an eastern idea. It was from the East that ancient Greece, in the years of her decline from the second century B.C. onwards, borrowed her various technical devices: before this, although possessing considerable scientific knowledge—including, moreover, a knowledge of machines and their utilization—there had been a persistent refusal to deduce or exploit the possible technical consequences. The Roman spirit, it may be said, was different from that of the Greeks, and sought to take advantage of concrete situations by the most effective practical means available; but even here the main technical processes—the refining of gold and silver, glass-making, the tempering of weapons, pottery, ship construction, and so on—were of eastern origin.

This lack of technical genius in the West or, rather, this refusal to admit technical exploitation except in a very limited sphere, was emphasized, not counteracted, by the spirit of Christianity. The period from the second century A.D. to the fifth century A.D. which saw the rise of Christianity, and which in Buddhist India was marked by astonishing developments in the artistic, political, military and technical fields, was marked in the West by a technical decline so great that the Emperor Julian the Apostate could accuse the Christians of ruining his Empire's industry. One of the architects of Hagia Sophia at Constantinople was quite capable of making a steam-engine (some 1200 years before James Watt 'invented' it), but he used his skill only to make the house he was living in shake as though there was an earthquake in order to get rid of an unpleasant neighbour living on the top floor. Except indeed for architecture—and nearly all large-scale architecture had a religious motive—the West in the mediaeval Christian period demonstrated a singular lack of technical will or mentality; and when in the twelfth century there was some renewal of technical interest this again was stimulated through contact with the East—through Jews, the Crusaders, Venetian and Genoese merchants, and through translations from the Arabic.

The West has developed technically in direct relationship to the decline of the Christian consciousness, for the simple reason that the 'secularization' of nature that permits it to be regarded as an object and so to be exploited technically, is in direct contradiction to the sacramental spirit of Christianity, wherever and whenever this is properly understood, as it was at least to some extent in the mediaeval world. Yet even after the breakdown of Christian authority in the West, technical development was slow: it was not until the eighteenth and nineteenth centuries that people began to think on any effective scale that the utilization of machines and gadgets in order to manipulate nature and to produce concrete results of a quantitative kind was a preoccupation not beneath the dignity of man.

It was the type of society of the mediaeval world along with its overriding orientation and pursuits that the scientific revolution destroyed. The new inorganic scientific order is man-made, not divine. It is one that represents indeed a projection of the human mind that has severed its links with the divine and with the earth. Its ideals, if they can be called that, are purely temporal and finite, and concern but the material well-being of its members. Its social forms are not the consequence of any supernatural revelation, but are simply the result of empirical and inductive methods of reasoning based primarily upon observation of individual needs and characteristics. These needs and characteristics are regarded as ultimately mortal: the ends of life are seen as contained within its mortal span and as measurable in terms of the purely temporal and finite standards of this world. Indeed, the finite world is regarded merely as finite: modern science is positive, which is to say that it views concrete material facts in isolation and stripped of all sacred quality. The awe and reverence induced by the recognition of the universal in the particular, of the divine in the human and natural, are alien to its discipline.

This new worldview, according to which man is basically a two-legged animal whose destiny and needs can best be fulfilled through the pursuit of social, political and economic self-interest, has been promoted, propagated and maintained, consciously or unconsciously, by generations of scientists from the seventeenth century down to the present day. Here of course Francis Bacon is a key figure, for it was Bacon who laid down the guidelines, moral, aesthetic and psychic, for the 'new philosophy'. When Bacon concluded that his *novum organum* should apply 'not only to natural but to all sciences' (including ethics and politics) and that it is to 'embrace everything', he opened the road for the all-inclusive scientific take-over of our culture and for the urban industrialism which is its brainchild.[33]

In Bacon's programme is to be found a prescription for the total scientivization of our world, from the practices of the laboratory, often themselves of an indescribable cruelty, down to those, no less sinister, of the modern police state. But if Bacon is the presiding genius, the *buccinator* of this take-over, it was others—Galileo, Descartes, Newton—who perfected that mechanistic vision in accordance with which our modern world has been built. It was they who marked the advent of a new conceptual universe, who formulated the purely quantitative attitude to nature which first appears in Galileo's new approach to terrestrial mechanics and who fostered the illusion that knowledge of the world could be obtained through the application of mathematical techniques—indeed, that whatever could not be caught in the net of numbers was non-science, non-knowledge and even in the end non-existent.

It was not Galileo but, as we have seen, Descartes who formulated most decisively the philosophical principles of the new science, its dream of reducing knowledge to mathematics, and of the new mathematical cosmology. Breaking the last tenuous links between God and the world He has created, Descartes virtually exiles God from the world—or, rather, exiles the world from God. For Descartes, God is no longer symbolized by the things He has created; his thought does not leave room even for the scholastic idea of analogy between God and the world: there are no *imagines* or *vestigia Dei in mundo*—except what Descartes calls the soul, which he identifies purely and simply with the human reason and the sparse complement of clear and distinct ideas with which God has endowed it. The Cartesian world is but a strictly uniform mathematical world, a world of geometry in which there is nothing else but extension and motion; and if God had any reasons for creating it, these are known only to Himself and we have not and cannot have the slightest idea of them or of any other divine or teleological realities, for the simple reason that, according to Descartes, we possess no faculty through which we are capable of apprehending them.

This of course meant the expulsion from scientific thought of all considerations based on value, perfection, harmony, meaning, beauty, purpose, for such considerations are now regarded as merely subjective and so as irrelevant to a scientific understanding of the real 'objective' world—the world of quantity, of reified geometry, of a nature that is impersonal and purely functional. With the Newtonian mechanistic synthesis, the new attitude is virtually achieved. The world-picture, with man in it, is flattened and neutralized, stripped of all sacred or spiritual qualities, of all hierarchical differentiation, and spread out before the human observer like a blank chart on which nothing can be registered except what is capable of being measured. For Newton, the celestial spheres are a machine, for Descartes, animals are machines, for Hobbes, society is a machine, for La Mettrie, the human body is a machine, eventually for Pavlov and his successors human behaviour is like that of a machine. There is nothing that is not reduced either to phenomenon (fact) or to mathematical hypothesis (or, in less polite language, fiction). The whole physical world is regarded as no more than so much inanimate dead matter whose chemical changes are mechanical processes based upon the so-called law of the conservation of mass. Everything, including the mind of man, is aligned on the model of a machine constructed out of dissections, analyses and calculations.

A worldview founded on the model of a machine brings after

it a mechanistic world. Already by the first half of the nineteenth century, if not earlier, scientists—and especially scientists who would apply their knowledge—were beginning to move into the centre of the social and economic scene. Aided and abetted by hard-headed industrialists and bankers possessed by a single-minded devotion to making money no matter what devastation they produced, scientists began to turn their expertise to the practical exploitation of the world's natural resources. It must be remembered, too, that they rode on the crest of the new 'spirit of the age'. There was a feeling of optimism in the air, a sense of moving forward into the future under the aegis of a new divinity, the Reason, that was now extending its empire over the whole western consciousness. Man was naturally good. The world was a good place to live in. It could be a much better place if only its natural resources and man's ability to put them to his use could be exploited more fully and efficiently.

This the scientists could do. They could do it by using their skills to develop the necessary techniques, the necessary technical means. In this way they would be in the forward van of humanity's march of progress towards a better and happier future. Scientists began to take the place of priests, initiating not of course into the kingdom of heaven but into the brave new world of more consumer goods and limitless economic growth. We who live in the throes of what we call the ecological crisis—which is primarily a crisis about man and not about his environment—are only too aware of how successful they have been for this to require any comment. All that need be said here is that as a result of their activity a new type of society has come into being: the society of the modern urban industrial and technological world.

For modern technology and its products are the scientific outlook harnessed and put to work for us. It is the capitulation of our society to the worldview of modern science that has licensed the technical mind to desecrate the whole social context, the entire planet, and to send out interminable squads of scientific-technical experts to chart, dissect, ransack, deface and ravage, dispassionately, on the basis of empirical evidence and experiment, and if possible by the intervention of mathematics or other specialist methodology, the total fabric of human and cosmic life—outer space and inner conflict, art and history, public opinion and private guilt, education and health—one has only to look at the hundreds of magazines and journals in the science departments of universities and polytechnics to get an idea of the vast proliferation of this specialized interference and scrutiny. Everything is drawn into this vortex of specialization and submitted to its processes. Nothing is sacrosanct. Nothing belongs any longer to the sphere of the gods or to the sphere of the supernatural. There is nothing and nowhere which must not be investigated and if possible exploited. Neither the ocean bed nor the stars can escape. Nor—so long as they can be shown to be efficient in the sense of being the best and most effective means for achieving certain measurable purposes, generally economic—can these systematic invasions be stopped or repudiated.

If efficient technical means for achieving something exist or can be produced, then these means must be put into action irrespective of what this thing is or of what the cost may be in human terms. Even those who were at first the victims of these processes—the industrial proletariat—have been seduced by their glamour and regard them as the magical talisman that will bring them all they need in life. As for the elite of our technocracy—those who manipulate its inexhaustible gadgetry of machines, devices, techniques, the computers and cybernated systems, the simulation and gaming processes, the market and motivational research, the immense codifications necessary to sustain and enlarge their empire of sterilized artificiality—their prestige is virtually unassailable because on them the whole edifice depends for its survival and prosperity. Moreover, if they are readers of Teilhard de Chardin, they can add ideological grist to their pragmatic mill, for he will have taught them that it is through the consolidation of the 'noosphere', that level of existence permanently dominated by the mind of man and its planning, that our species will execute its God-given task and fulfil its destiny.[34]

There is, however, a price to be paid for fabricating around us a society which is as artificial and as mechanized as our own, and this is that we can exist in it only on condition that we adapt ourselves to it. This is our punishment. The social form that we have adopted cuts our consciousness to fit its needs, its imperatives tailor our experience. The inorganic technological world that we have invented lays hold of our interior being and seeks to reduce that to a blind inorganic mechanical thing. It seeks to eliminate whole emotional areas of our life, demanding that we be a new type of being, a type that is not human as this has been understood in the religious and even in the humanist conception of things—one that has no heart, no affections, no spontaneity, and is as impersonal as the metals and processes of calculation in which it is involved.

Moreover, it is not only our emotional world that is deadened. The world of our creative imagination and intelligence is also impoverished. The most average characterless type of mind is quite sufficient to master and apply the various skills, scientific and other, needed to run our society. At the same time, the objects which we now make or manufacture require little or no imaginative effort on our part; they are all the result of rational planning and design, of technical skill and efficiency, and we produce them—are forced to produce them—with the least possible personal struggle or commitment, entering into and becoming through producing them part of their objective, impersonal and pitiless nature. For these products—machines, commodities, organizations, programmes—are themselves totally devoid of any imaginative quality: they mirror nothing which is not material, they are symbols of nothing, they are entirely consumed by their own lifeless and inorganic indifference; and man who must spend his days among them is reduced to a similar state.

Indeed, what goes by the name of work for the vast majority of the members of our society rots the very soul and body. It is work which takes no account whatsoever of the personal qualities of the individuals engaged in it; it has no direct connection with what a particular person really is or with that by virtue of which he is himself and not someone else; it is purely external to him and he can exchange it—if there is anything available—for an alternative which is equally impersonal and exterior. In relation to our work, the vast majority of us in our society are equivalent to mere 'units', or objects or commodities, and are condemned for all our working lives to purely mechanical activities in which nothing properly human exists and whose performance is not in any way consistent with our inner and personal aptitudes and identities.

When it is remembered that if an individual does not fulfil the function for which he is destined by nature and which is his vocation, but is forced to perform some other function, not essentially connected with him, then he will produce in himself a dislocation and disharmony which affects the whole society to which he belongs, something of the sickness of our state may be grasped. For in our society, that is not the exception, it is the rule; and in these circumstances the dislocation affects not merely society, but the whole cosmic realm itself. It is superfluous to stress that this cosmic disorder, reflecting the radical dehumanization of our society, and incurable apart from a total repersonalization of the conditions of work in our society, is already well advanced. As the conditions of work, and above all the type of work itself—for it is this that is crucial—cannot be repersonalized or rehumanized without a dismantling of the whole present scientific industrial structure, we have something of the measure of the task that lies ahead.

At this point I would like to forestall a possible criticism, especially as by so doing I will reach what is the crux of my whole argument: the question of why subscription to the modern scientific outlook inevitably results in the dehumanization of man. It might be said that the mechanistic worldview which I am here identifying with that of modern science has long since been discarded by scientists themselves, relegated to that rubbish-dump of exploded theories which constitutes the history of modern science. The quantum and relativity theories proposed at the turn of the twentieth century might be cited in support of this claim that the scientific worldview has radically changed.

In addition, it could be pointed out that philosophers of science like Ernst Mach or Henri Poincaré—to mention but two of the more intelligent positivists—have shown that the theories and explanatory concepts of science are no more than convenient intellectual tools by means of which scientists handle their data and reduce it to comparative order, and that they should be valued for their utility and convenience only and not as statements of truth about reality. Mach certainly, and Poincaré probably, would go on to say that there are no ultimate truths about reality in any case, although those of science are as near as any we are likely to get. And more recently, other philosophers of science like Michael Polanyi have spoken of how impossible it is for the scientist not to be influenced by purely subjective factors such as what he expects to see, what other people have persuaded him that he should see, and so on—factors which mean that measurements of temporal and spatial intervals are not just given to the mind but are given to a particular mind deeply and inextricably involved with its own subjective personal prejudices and requirements.[35]

In short, it could be argued that scientists themselves now admit that the best of their theories are but hypotheses, and that these, far from being reached inductively on the basis of objective data, as the old-fashioned empiricist would have it, are for the most part simply postulated as the most probable explanation or interpretation of certain data in accordance with a specific model which the scientist in question happens to have accepted. Thus, Le Verrier postulated by purely mathematical means the then unknown planet Neptune, or more recently Watson and Crick proceeded in a similar manner when developing their theory of the genetic code. All this, it might be concluded, means that the old closed, rigid, cast-iron mechanistic picture of the universe, in which man was seen as a mere cog in a vast cosmic machine, has now gone forever, and that science, the new science, is open, flexible, indefinite and much more aware of its limitations than was previously the case. Indeed, it is even thought, both by some scientists and by some theologians, that it might now be possible to reconcile science and religion in a new religio-scientific conception of things.

Some of this is no doubt true, just as it is no doubt true that many scientists, aware of the crushing inhumanity of their discipline, are desperately looking for something which would appear to allow the human and even the religious element to be affirmed within it. For a whole range of phenomena in atomic physics and astronomy the old machine model is inadequate and scientists working in these areas are forced to revise their observational methods, to invent new and more flexible models, and to develop more subtle mathematical procedures for construing their experimental data.

Indeed, some scientists—and among them perhaps Fritjof Capra is the most popular spokesman[36]—claim that what they call the new physics has entirely emancipated itself from the mechanistic worldview of Cartesian and Newtonian physics and has in fact moved close to the worldview of Eastern mysticism. The two basic theories of modern physics—the quantum theory and the theory of relativity—exhibit, it is claimed, all the main features of the Eastern worldview. Quantum theory has abolished the old notion of fundamentally separated objects, has introduced the concept of participator to replace that of observer, and has come to see the universe as an interconnected web of relations whose parts are only defined through their connections to the whole. Relativity theory has made the cosmic web come alive by revealing its intrinsically dynamic character, by showing that its activity is the very essence of its being. As a result of this the universe is now seen as a dynamic web of interrelated events. None of the properties of any part of this web is fundamental: each follows from the properties of the other parts, and the overall consistency of their mutual interrelations determines the structure of the entire web.

In fact of course none of this represents a breakaway from the basic conceptual framework underlying modern science; and if proof for this is needed it can be found in the fact that the three theories which the 'new physics' takes as axiomatic (in spite of their being by definition no more than hypotheses) and which entirely condition its formulations—namely the two already specified (the quantum theory and the relativity theory) and the theory of evolution which goes with them—are all merely inevitable logical developments from the premises that constitute the basic conceptual framework of modern science. Nothing fundamental has shifted with respect to the acceptance of these premises: they are as unquestioned as they ever have been, and the much-vaunted 'new physics' is no more than the old physics in a new guise.

Moreover, in its own way the 'new physics' is no less deterministic and mechanistic than the old physics: you don't escape from determinism and mechanicalness simply by altering the way in which you conceive the relationship between the parts of the physical cosmos unless simultaneously you recognize a non-determined and undeterminable principle of relationship that altogether transcends both this cosmos and *a fortiori* the realm of scientific enquiry itself; and in the case of the 'new physics' no such principle is recognized and it is still assumed that what happens in the sphere of atomic and sub-atomic events is governed by statistical laws that can be expressed in mathematical terms. All that has occurred is that the notion of causality of the old physics, which applied to objects and events in isolation, has now been replaced by a concept of statistical causality in which the probabilities for atomic events are determined by the dynamics of the whole system: we are simply in a bigger cage.

Ultimately, if the 'new physics' has performed any positive service it is that it demonstrates more clearly than ever before the total incompetence of modern science to say anything about the nature of the universe in which one can place any trust at all. The corollary of the notion that the properties of any part of this universe are determined by the properties of all the other parts, is that in order to understand any single phenomenon we have to understand all the others as well. As this is a total impossibility, physicists have to accept that in the nature of things their knowledge at best is only approximate and in the end, if they could take into account more phenomena than in practice they can possibly take into account, may even turn out to be utterly mistaken and hence not knowledge at all but merely an aberration.

Thus their attempt to explain many phenomena by their examination of a few is a purely arbitrary process and cannot have anything to do with knowledge in the real sense of the word. Yet this on their own confession is all they are capable of doing: that all scientific theories and models are by definition approximations, and may be totally inadequate to convey a true picture of the reality with which they purport to be dealing, is a conclusion to which all modern scientific research is condemned by the premises from which it starts.

Perhaps nothing so indicates the impasse into which modern

science has been driven as what its exponents claim to be one of the chief signs of its progress, namely, the recognition that the consciousness of the observer (or participator) is an essential aspect of the conclusion he draws about the nature of physical phenomena. Apart from the fact that this is something that could have been learnt from any spiritual or metaphysical tradition worthy of the name, it lands scientists themselves, given their premises, in a completely non-sensical position.

For if human consciousness plays a crucial role in the process of observation, to such an extent that my decision about how I observe an electron, for instance, will determine the properties which I actually attribute to it, it must follow that until I know what consciousness is and what are the characteristics and limitations of the type of consciousness with which I observe, I am powerless to assess in what manner my consciousness has determined the properties I am capable of observing in a particular phenomenon, or to what degree what I observe simply reflects my own consciousness but otherwise has little or nothing to do with anything one can call reality. Indeed, if—as the new physicists admit—every change of consciousness alters what is observed, all the modern scientist is doing when he propounds theories is merely 'objectifying' in the conventional language of his discipline the limitations of his own individual consciousness. Had he possessed a higher degree of consciousness than the one he actually possesses, he would see things in quite a different light and so conclude with quite another understanding of them, an understanding that he might find it quite impossible to express in the language of mathematics.

All this makes it more than clear that the 'new physics' is just as trapped as the old physics in a conceptual framework from which it can escape only by recognizing what by now should be self-evident, namely, the utter insufficiency of its premises. In any case, whatever the claims, however spurious, now made by scientists for the 'new physics', the old physics is still to all intents and purposes the physics of an equally wide range of phenomena, of all those phenomena which belong to what might be called our local environment, of ordinary space and ordinary time.

Where the so-called life-sciences are concerned, scientific

thought is in fact more crudely mechanistic than ever. In biology, the cell is a 'chemical factory', ribosomes are directed by a 'programming machine', DNA is like 'a worker in a multicopying industry who duplicates the programme of an automatic machine on the keyboard of a key punch', and so on. 'In science,' as Joseph Needham put it, 'a man is a machine, or if he is not, then he is nothing';[37] and as if to confirm his words, and to illustrate what I have said already to the effect that the type of mind needed for science can be the most average and characterless from the point of view of normal human intelligence, Francis Crick, the Nobel prizewinner, discoverer of the bihelical structure of DNA, can write: 'I myself, like many scientists, believe that the soul is imaginary and that what we call our mind is simply a way of talking about the functions of our brains'; and can add: 'once one has become adjusted to the idea that we are here because we have evolved from simple chemical compounds by a process of natural selection, it is remarkable how many of the problems of the modern world take on a completely new light.'[38]

The real reason, however, invalidating the claim that the modern scientific outlook is fundamentally different from that of Galileo, Descartes and Newton, and so is more susceptible to humanization, goes much deeper than this continuing adherence to the machine metaphor. Scientists may well dispense with this metaphor and adopt some other in its place. That is not fundamentally very significant. But what they cannot do without admitting their total insufficiency is to dispense with the premisses, or presuppositions, on which modern science itself is based. And by premisses I mean epistemological assumptions, the conceptual framework of the mind within which the modern scientist works, whether he is aware of it or not.

Modern scientists may concede that their theories are mere hypotheses, more or less useful and convenient. They may admit that the old empiricist epistemology—according to which knowledge can be obtained only on the basis of observation—was inadequate and even false, and that into any act of observation and any formulation of theory enter factors—hereditary, cultural, subjective—which the scientist cannot specify and of which indeed he may be largely unaware. But unless they are to confess to a complete inner conversion they cannot reject the very premisses of modern scientific thought itself. And these premisses—these underlying premisses—are the same today as they were for the scientists of the seventeenth century. And the reason why scientists, short of the conversion of which I have spoken, cannot humanize science is because inhumanity is built into the very premisses on which modern science is based.

It is here that we approach the crux of the matter. It may seem presumptuous to try to indicate the premisses of modern scientific knowledge in a few sentences. But I think it can be done. Basically, scientific theories, hypotheses or explanations are statements which either can be verified with reference to empirical evidence or experiment, or at least cannot be shown to be false with reference to such evidence or experiment. In other words, scientific knowledge presupposes two terms or poles. The first is the faculty that actually formulates scientific statements; and the second is an 'objective' world of phenomena that supplies the raw material of evidence and experiment against which these statements can be directly or indirectly checked. This is not to say that these two terms are symmetrical or of equal importance. It is only to say that they are posited as the prerequisites of scientific knowledge. Without either, there could be no knowledge as modern science understands the word.

In fact, it is quite clear that the two terms are not symmetrical or of equal importance. It is the first—that which I have called the faculty that actually formulates scientific statements—which is decisive. It is decisive not only because it is the formulating agent but also because it is the faculty that observes and that provides the criteria determining what is observed, as well as the criteria of the relevance or irrelevance, the compatibility or incompatibility of the information it amasses as a result of its observations. Indeed, it is this faculty alone that is the supreme arbiter of scientific knowledge. It is therefore crucial, if one is to appraise the value of this knowledge, to know what this faculty itself is, as well as the criteria according to which it assesses and evaluates its material; for what it is and the standards that govern its activity will determine the whole character of its formulations.

Here I would refer again to a distinction, made in the opening chapter of this book, between two inter-related faculties in man, the spiritual intellect and the reason; and would now specify, as indeed became explicit at the conclusion of the last chapter, that the faculty by which modern science is determined is not the spiritual intellect, with its capacity for apprehending and experiencing metaphysical and eternal realities, but the reason, which in itself is incapable of apprehending and experiencing such realities. The question before us, therefore, is one of distinguishing the characteristics of the reason, and of perceiving the nature of the standards to which it refers in carrying out the role that modern scientists have assigned to it; for it tends to be axiomatic among scientists that their discipline is a rational one, or at least more so than other disciplines, and that its form of knowledge is correspondingly a rational form, so that it is important to see in what sense this is the case.

The reason is that faculty which is capable of dissecting, analyzing and classifying material, and of forming conclusions by means of analytical or analogical logic, measurement and mechanical connection. But the conclusions it forms as a result of its activity will not be merely arbitrary; on the contrary, they will depend upon the framework of conceptions within which the reason operates, because it is these conceptions that provide it with the criteria according to which it assesses and interprets the material with which it is presented. This is to say that the scope of the reason is limited on the one hand by the material with which it is presented and on the other by the conceptions in the light of which it assesses this material although they do not necessarily arise from it. The reason knows this material only according to how it appears to it and not as it is in itself, and similarly it knows the conceptions only as logical possibilities and not as realities in themselves.

As for the conceptions, or presuppositions, that form the framework within which the reason operates and that provide the reason with the criteria for its interpretations and evaluations, these are not simply intrinsic to the reason as such nor, contrary to what often appears to be assumed, are some more rational than others. They are the starting-points, so to speak, that the reason has to accept or adopt, consciously or unconsciously, *a priori* as a condition of its functioning at all. In this sense they are extrinsic to the reason, and escape its control in as much as their reality or unreality, truth or falsehood, are not susceptible to rational or logical proof or demonstration. In other words, they are articles of faith, though not necessarily of faith in spiritual or metaphysical realities; and the reason's competence with respect to them consists at most in its capacity to accept or reject adherence to one particular conceptual framework rather than to another.

This being the case, the reason may derive the conceptions according to which it operates either from 'above', from the metaphysical or spiritual world, in which case they will be mediated to it directly through the intellect's apprehension of this world or indirectly through the revealed scriptures of a particular religious tradition and the inspired writings of its recognized spiritual masters; or it may derive them in a more or less arbitrary fashion from the cogitations of individuals or groups of individuals that formulate them without reference to any spiritual source of knowledge. In this latter case, they will be purely subjective, having no more authority or authenticity than that which other individuals, again on purely subjective grounds, choose to accord to them or to those who put them forth.

As we have already seen, the conceptual framework within which the modern scientific mentality operates is not one that presupposes adherence to a particular religious doctrine or illumination from a spiritual source of knowledge. On the contrary, it is derived from the body of philosophical ideas whose development and character we have surveyed in the preceding chapter and which may be said to have found its representative spokesmen in figures like Descartes and his peers. It is a body of ideas that posits first that the reason is the supreme faculty of knowledge and second that the conclusions of the reason may be quite valid without reference to any scriptural or revealed principles of knowledge, even when they contradict the latter. Indeed, it further maintains that the conclusions of the reason may be declared to be invalid only when they contradict the empirical evidence of sense-data or sense-impression, or of experiment carried out in relation to the phenomenal world.

This has meant in practice that the modern scientific mentality not only does not recognize the authority and authenticity of any supra-individual body of knowledge from which it derives its conceptual framework and hence the criteria according to which it forms its conclusions; it is also radically dependent on information supplied through observation of the phenomenal world. As this world is by definition a world of change and impermanence, it follows that the conclusions formed on the basis of its observation cannot themselves be other than relative to what is changing and impermanent, and hence will have the same provisional character. It is no accident that among current theories of modern science one is that of evolution, another is that of relativity and a third is that of indeterminacy.

From this it will be apparent that although one may say that modern science is rational in so far as its conclusions follow logically from its initial presuppositions, one cannot say that it is in the least rational with respect to the actual decision to adopt these presuppositions rather than any others in the first place. In other words, modern science, in spite of its appeal to rational categories, is ultimately no more—and no less—rational than any other structure of belief that from a given framework of accepted presuppositions permits certain conclusions to be drawn by means of logical analysis and deduction. It is in this respect no more—and no less—rational than any form of dogmatic religion. What is particular about it is that its presuppositons so rigorously preclude spiritual values and principles from determining its interpretations and understandings of human and other life.

For modern science has its starting-point in a revolution in consciousness, or revolt against heaven, that has resulted in the reason first ignoring, then denying and finally closing itself to spiritual sources of knowledge; and this has meant that it has been forced to adopt presuppositions of a non-spiritual and purely individual kind and to apply criteria implicit in them in its investigation and analysis of data supplied by the phenomenal world. Moreover, the reason is not, and cannot be, a neutral element or *tabula rasa* on to which the objects of this world can project themselves in such a way that they reveal their own intrinsic nature. Rather the opposite is the case: what the reason perceives in an object will simply reflect that which its own conceptual framework and its own inherent character allow it to perceive.

This is to say that when the reason, unillumined by any spiritual or metaphysical principles of knowledge, turns to the phenomenal world for information, not only will that which it perceives be conditioned by its own accepted presuppositions, whatever these may happen to be, but also in analyzing and classifying that which it perceives it will take account only of those aspects that are susceptible to measurement and mechanical connection. Any aspects not susceptible to measurement and mechanical connection must in the nature of things escape the grasp of the reason, and so cannot enter into the conclusions it forms on the basis of its observation. In other words, the reason cannot avoid imposing its own limitations on the material that it perceives.

In fact, these limitations act as a selector determining what it perceives and what it does not perceive. Hence it is that in interrogating the phenomenal world—in interrogating the 'facts of nature'—what the reason receives by way of information will be, so to speak, simply the echoes of its own voice. Indeed, the conclusions it forms as a result of its analysis and classification of sense-data according to the criteria it has adopted and according to its inherent mode of operation will represent little more than a display of ventriloquism in which the phenomenal world takes the part of the dummy. Nor is the situation altered by the addition of instruments interposed between the reason and the objects that it observes: however sophisticated and sensitive the instrument, the information it conveys cannot transcend or escape the limitations of the actual observing faculty itself.

This is why the kind of knowledge that the reason is now capable of forming on the basis of its observation is but a reflection of its own intrinsic characteristics and of the non-spiritual presuppositions it has adopted, and has little or nothing to do with what things are in themselves, in their living reality. Indeed, all the reason can now do is to shut man up in himself and fetter him to his own prejudices and opinions and condemn him to rest satisfied with what at best are but the external appearances of things. What things are in themselves, in their living reality, is something beyond its grasp.

It is because of this that modern science, based as it is on a rationality subordinated to non-spiritual categories, likewise can never attain a knowledge of anything in itself, no matter how much it concerns itself with experiment and observation or how far it carries its function of dissection and analysis. This is the situation to which modern science has been condemned and in which it continues to be trapped. It is compelled by its very premises to ignore in things those qualities that transcend their finite appearance and the reason's capacity for logical analysis and deduction.

Yet, as we saw in the opening chapter of this book, it is essentially such qualities that, from the Christian point of view, make a human being what he or she is. For we saw in that chapter how from this point of view that which essentially constitutes the humanity of a human being is participation in the divine; and that to base an assessment of man on the assumption that he is to be understood apart from these inherently divine or spiritual qualities that constitute his essential nature and make him a human being will be to conclude with conceptions that effectively reduce him to a subhuman or even an inhuman status. It will be effectively to dehumanize man.

Yet this is what the modern scientific mentality is bound to do, since its assessment of man is based precisely on such an assumption. Indeed, one may go further and say that the whole conceptual framework within which modern science is conducted precludes any understanding of man other than that which must debase him in this way. This is why it may be affirmed that inhumanity is built into the very premisses on which modern science itself is based. This, too, is why the forms of life, social and other, developed in accordance with the modern scientific understanding of man do in fact end in dehumanizing him. As these forms dominate our world, we perceive the scope of the mutilation of human life with which as a consequence we are inevitably faced.

This is not of course to say that the reason cannot have a positive function or that there can be no science of phenomena. Far from it. But when on the *ipse dixit* of some philosopher or group of philosophers the reason is set up as the arbiter of human knowledge and denies or ignores principles and qualities of a spiritual nature, then it necessarily degenerates into a mechanical, inhuman and godless faculty; and the picture of the universe that it projects and the character of the world that it fabricates in accordance with that picture will be equally mechanical, inhuman and godless.

None of this would be very important if modern science, like chess or trapeze artistry, was but the pursuit of a few specialists. Unfortunately, this is not the case. Whether we like it or not, the scientific attitude has permeated and vitally affected virtually every aspect of our public and private thinking and action. It is not simply that our governments pour enormous sums of money annually through schools, universities, research projects and multitudinous other ways, into its promotion and dissemination. It is more serious than that. The scientific conception of knowledge has become virtually equated with the only way of knowing there is. Not only does it dominate its own offspring, such as the social sciences and anthropology, but it has invaded also the classical fields of the humanities, a fact which makes a proper understanding of poetry, for instance, almost inaccessible to the modern student. The degree to which philosophy has capitulated is clear from the extent to which it is preoccupied with such mental gymnastics as logical analysis and even mere information theory.

Far more serious, however, is the capitulation of theology, the one discipline that should from the start have exposed the limitations of the modern scientific mentality. More will be said about this in the following chapter.[39] Here it is sufficient to remark that, taking refuge in a supposition, proposed by St Thomas Aquinas[40] and re-affirmed by philosophers such as Kant, to the effect that although the reason can have no direct apprehension of the realities of revelation in themselves, nevertheless its mode of cognition and its conclusions are quite valid with respect to the phenomenal world—the world of nature—

theologians for the most part have lulled themselves into a completely false security. Even worse, they have felt obliged to modify their own doctrine where this has run counter to the various theories which scientists have put forward from time to time about the origin of the universe, the evolution of man and so on. Because of this they have been led into the absurd situation of trying to bring Christian doctrine up to date or to remake it in accordance with the spirit of the times or with the contemporary mind, quite forgetting that this up-to-dateness, this spirit of the times and this contemporary mind are for the most part determinations of a science which by definition is destructive of the religious intelligence and its norms.

The result has been that theologians have largely failed to make any radical or effective critique of scientific epistemology, to elucidate the consequences of making the reason the supreme and sole instrument of knowledge, and to explain why this has meant a progressive falsification of our understanding both of ourselves and of the world about us. In view of this failure it is not surprising that so many students of our universities end up with no better ideology than some form of Marxist-Leninism, itself a translation into political terms of some of the most banal aspects of nineteenth century bourgeois scientific theory. When this same hotch-potch of rationalist-materialist constructs is taken over by—or, rather, takes possession of—the masses, then society is turned into a prison-camp in which everything that gives human life its value and dignity is systematically attacked and lacerated.

At this point—if not indeed at some much earlier point—it might be objected that the picture that is being drawn is too bleak and that things are not as bad as they are being made to appear. First, it could be said that even if in general terms the description made here of the effects of submitting to the categories of the scientific mentality is true with reference to certain spheres of activity, none the less in other spheres there have been such positive gains that these offset, if they do not outweigh, any disadvantages; and that in any case these disadvantages themselves can be corrected when we have a little more knowledge about them. In particular, it might be claimed that the gains in the field of medicine are so vast that these alone

[86]

justify the whole scientific experiment of the last few centuries.

I do not think it is so simple. The world of modern science—and this includes the world of techniques and technicians that has developed within it—is a single interlocking whole and it is impossible to abstract one aspect of it as if this aspect could exist independently of the other aspects. It is impossible to do this because any one process, however beneficial it may seem in itself, is inextricably involved with a thousand other processes and depends upon them. If you want a product such as a car you have to have all the rest as well, from the dereliction of the oil-rigs, the refineries and the motorways down to the lead poison, the carbon monoxide and the noise that ruins the life of our cities, as well as the deadly boredom of those whose task it is to put these machines together. In any case, it is surely inappropriate to acclaim, say, medicine when the type of mind and society which it presupposes is one that has done so much to deprive man of the basic elements on which his health depends. It should be added that more and more scientists are becoming aware of this kind of dilemma into which the pursuit of their discipline has led them. Whether or not this growing awareness will initiate a radical change of mind and direction it is too early to know. One can only hope that it will.

Beyond this, however, it may be questioned whether the scientific takeover is quite so totalitarian as I have suggested. In the sphere of the intelligence and the imagination, there have always been those who have resisted its claims: poets, for instance, such as Blake, who discerned so clearly to where the thought of Bacon, Locke and Newton would lead; or Yeats, who hated this science and called it 'the opium of the suburbs'; or Eric Gill and David Jones, who knew so well that when man's work is merely utilitarian it is also sub-human and how in the technological world man's capacity to make—his function as *poeta*—is brutalized out of recognition.[41] The testimony of these four alone—and there are many others—is sufficient to indicate that the creative intelligence and imagination, necessarily anti-scientific, have not been extinguished. Indeed, the smell of the rose is still as much the smell of the rose for us as it was for Plato and, in spite of all, our lives are still punctuated by moments of grace, beauty and love that give us intimations of realities that lie far beyond all I have been talking about. In this sense, everything is still in its place and nothing has been lost. In fact, since the worldview of modern science is basically false, it cannot ultimately affect the truth of things, however much it may appear to do so. The norm of human and natural existence always remains.

Moreover, it may be maintained that throughout his history man has always been willing to despoil his natural environment in order to satisfy his needs and greeds; and although modern technology has permitted us to do this on a scale hitherto unprecedented, so that we are now threatened with global catastrophes which will destroy all our present forms of civilization as well as the greater part of the human race, we must not on this account underestimate nature's own intrinsic powers of recuperation. In addition, awareness of the problems which confront us with respect to such environmental degradation as the destruction of the tropical rainforest, rapidly increasing overpopulation and desertification, the excessive use and abuse of energy and resources, or the terrifying magnitude of the aesthetic and physical pollution within which we are forced to live, is already producing remedial reaction and action on the part of man himself, often with positive effect.[42]

All this is undoubtedly true, and—as we shall reaffirm in the Epilogue—we demean ourselves and our potentialities when we take an unrelievedly pessimistic view of our fate. Yet equally we demean ourselves when we nourish ourselves on illusions. The social and cultural order that we have built and are continuing to build about us—our present—is one predominantly determined by the categories of a false philosophy and its practical application; and the consequence of our acquiescence on such a mass scale to what amounts to a lie about ourselves and the true nature of the physical world cannot but be an increasing divorce between this order and that of the human and natural norm. In fact, this divorce has now become so great that it is virtually impossible for the one to understand the other. We have all but lost the capacity to measure how far we have in fact fallen below the level of the human and natural norm.

For modern science has its origin in a loss of memory, a

forgetfulness by man of who he is. By an ineluctable logic inherent in this origin it proceeds along a course each step of which is marked by a further fall by man into deeper ignorance of his own nature and consequently into deeper ignorance of the nature of everything else. Progressively divorced by this ignorance from the roots of his being, man, so long as he persists in this course, is doomed to advance blindly and at an ever-increasing pace towards total loss of identity, total loss of control and eventually to total self-destruction. Nothing can stop this process except a complete reversal of direction. And nothing can initiate a reversal of direction except a recovery by man of an awareness of who he is: the cure must go back to where the sickness started.

To such a recovery modern science, unless it radically shifts its premisses, can contribute nothing: a science whose very categories exclude a recognition of the essential qualities of human nature clearly is not in a position to make man the subject of its investigation with any hope of telling us anything very important about him. Only a religious understanding of man—one that is aware of these essential qualities—is capable of restoring what has been lost and so of at least beginning to set right what has been made so drastically wrong. It is something of such an understanding that I have endeavoured to explore in the opening chapter of this book. It remains to explore a similar understanding in relation to the world of nature and to show how its eclipse has had consequences in that world which correspond to the processes of dehumanization that we have been examining in this present chapter.

4

The Desanctification of Nature

IN THE PRECEDING chapters attention has been concentrated above all on the theme of man and on the shifts in the Christian and post-Christian understanding which have resulted in what we have described as his eclipse. But running alongside this theme, and indeed overlapping it and intertwined with it, is another, which concerns man's attitude to nature. We have frequently had occasion to note how our understanding of man is intimately related to our understanding of nature. Indeed, so much is this the case that our failure to perceive the divine in man has gone hand in hand with a failure to perceive the divine in nature. As we have dehumanized man, so we have desanctified nature. Yet although these two themes are inextricably interconnected, and although in what sense this is so has already been more than indicated, so that to elaborate further may involve a certain degree of repetition, none the less the theme of the desanctification of nature is itself so important that it deserves independent consideration.

By the phrase, 'the desanctification of nature', I refer to that process whereby the spiritual significance and understanding of the created world has been virtually banished from our minds, and we have come to look upon things and creatures as though they possessed no sacred or numinous quality. It is a process which has accustomed us to regard the created world as composed of so many blind forces, essentially devoid of meaning, personality and grace, which may be investigated, used, manipulated and consumed for our own scientific or economic interest. In short, it has led us to see the world only as so much secularized or desacralized material, with the consequence that we have ruptured the organic links and spiritual equilibrium between man and nature, and have restricted religion more and more to the privacy of the individual conscience or to concern for the beyond of a transcendent God or of an individual salvation after earthly existence is over.

This does not mean of course that people have stopped finding a charm or a beauty in nature, or an outlet from the artificial and suffocating atmosphere of our over-industrialized cities. On the contrary, from the eighteenth century onwards our history has been characterized by periodic 'back to nature' movements, as if nature was a kind of unspoilt paradise ready with ever-open arms to compensate man for all the other losses he has suffered. But what this so often represents is the romantic or sentimental reaction of an exhausted and disillusioned individualism, containing in it very little that may be described as spiritual. In fact, it can very well go, and very often has gone, with an entirely 'atheist' outlook. What is in question here is not this kind of naturalism, but a loss of the sense of the divine in nature—a loss of the sense that the very stuff of the universe has a sacred quality. In what follows I shall try to say something of how this situation has come about and what it means.

There has been a growing tendency within the post-mediaeval Christian world to look upon creation as the artifact of a Maker who as it were has produced it from without. This has provided us with a picture of a God in heaven who, having set the cosmic process in motion and having left it to run more or less on its own and according to its own laws, now interferes directly on but rare occasions and then only in the form of special and 'abnormal' acts operated upon the world from without. The result is that the relation between God and creation tends to be seen predominantly as one of cause and effect: God is a world cause, a supreme or first cause or principle of being; and the world and its laws are what He has produced.

On this account, it may be possible to speak of some analogy between God and creation. It may be possible to say that creation is a 'moving image of eternity', a kind of projection in corruptible terms of its unmoved perfection, or even that signs and indications of God may be discerned in visible phenomena. But what is difficult to envisage in this perspective is the idea that creation actually participates in the divine, and is an actual mode of existence or embodiment of the living, ever-present God.

I would call this idea that creation is the embodiment of the divine—with its rider that all nature has therefore an intrinsically sacred character—the sacramental idea of creation. This would appear appropriate because what is implied in this idea is that the Christian understanding of sacrament, which is usually applied only to the specific rites that go by the name of sacraments in the institutional Church, is applied to the realm of nature as a whole.

A sacrament, it must be remembered, demands a material expression. In fact, the archetype of all sacramental activity is the Incarnation of Christ Himself. In the Incarnation, the Logos becomes flesh: there is an intimate meeting and inextricable intertwining of the spiritual and the material. As we have already noted, what is defended or affirmed in the great Christological discussions which resulted in the pronouncements of Nicaea and Chalcedon is that the two natures in Christ—the divine and the human, the uncreated and the created—are not merely juxtaposed in the person of Christ. There is not simply an assumption by the divine of the human. These ways of regarding the mystery of the two natures in Christ are felt to be inadequate and to fail to do justice to its reality. What is defended or afffirmed is the actual union of the two natures—a union 'without confusion, without change, without division, without separation', as the formula of the Council of Chalcedon puts it. In other words, it is maintained that however vast and fundamental the difference between the uncreated and the created may appear, there is ultimately no radical dichotomy between them. If God is God, and if God is manifest in Christ, then creation must be capable of becoming one with the uncreated and it must be possible to transcend the apparent ontological gap between them.

This is why when the Greek Fathers speak of the Eucharist, which is the image of the Incarnation—and it must be remembered that for the Greek Fathers the only difference between image and archetype is that the image as such is not the archetype as such—they insist that the material sign of the sacrament is not simply something to which the Spirit is attached, as if the Spirit were an extraneous element added to the matter, or one that 'transubstantiates' the matter through His presence. On the contrary, they insist that there is a total integration of the material and the spiritual, so that the elements of bread and wine are an actual mode of existence of the divine and there is a complete union between them.

In other words, the sacrament presupposes an actual incarnation of divine power and life; and what is communicated to man in the sacrament is this divine power and life. As St Cyril of Alexandria puts it: 'For the Son is in us on the one hand bodily, as man, united and mixed by means of the Eucharist (mystical blessing); and also spiritually, as God, by the energy and grace of His own Spirit renewing the spirit that is in us for the renewal of life and making us participants in His divinity'.[43]

It is now possible to see the consequence of applying the Christian understanding of the sacrament to the realm of nature as a whole. It means that nature is regarded not as something upon which God acts from without. It is regarded as something through which God expresses Himself from within. Nature, or creation (the terms are interchangeable in this context), is perceived as the self-expression of the divine, and the divine as totally present within it. It is not a case of complete absorption of the one in the other, or of subservience on the one side and detachment on the other. Moreover, the created depends for its existence on the uncreated, while the uncreated does not depend in the least for its existence on the created. But each finds its own identity in the other, and each at the same time keeps its own identity in the other.

In creating what is created, it is Himself that God creates, in another mode. In creation He becomes His own image, in such a way that He enters into it from within. He is its within. Creation is the realm in which God's dynamic, pulsating energies are made manifest. Its apparent stability is simply the flux of these energies, its solidity the result of their ceaseless flow. In this respect the difference between the activity of the Spirit in nature and the activity of the Spirit outside nature is one of degree only, not of kind: it is a difference of the mode in which

[93]

the Spirit operates while the energies through which He operates remain always divine and uncreated.

Like the Eucharist, nature is a revelation not merely of the truth about God but of God Himself. The created world is God's sacrament of Himself to Himself in His creatures: it is the means whereby He is what He is. Were there no creation, then God would be other than He is; and if creation were not sacramental, then God would not be its creator and there would be no question of a sacrament anywhere. If God is not present in a grain of sand then He is not present in heaven either.

It is, then, this sacramental idea of nature which has been eliminated from our minds in order to permit that process of desanctification about which I have spoken. I say 'from our minds' advisedly, because the fact that we do not 'see God in all things' and sense His presence everywhere does not mean that He is not in all things and is not present everywhere. Reality is what it is, and so is revelation. That we fail to perceive them as what they are means that we have lost sight of them, not that the structure of reality has changed. The secular has its origin in man's loss of spiritual vision or—what is the same thing—in the hardening of his heart; and the contraction of the world of nature to a self-contained entity, which is what happens when we ignore its sacred aspect, represents not so much a closing off of nature itself as a closing of our own eyes. We always have to remember that how we see the world about us is but a reflection of the state of our own inner world. Ultimately it is because we see ourselves as existing apart from God that we also see nature as existing apart from God.

This last statement is to the point here because what the modern scientific outlook and the building of our modern technological and economic order demonstrate is the triumph of precisely the view in which the world is seen as a self-contained entity, existing in its own right, apart from God, and consequently as something that man is quite entitled to explore, organize and exploit without any reference to the divine. As we have seen, the modern secular world owes its immediate origin not so much to the Renaissance and Reformation or to Copernicus and Galileo as to the scientific revolution of the seventeenth century, with its 'New Philosophy', as the scientists of the seventeenth century themselves called it.

In its turn, this revolution may be said to have two main characteristics, which are closely interconnected. The first is that it assumed that knowledge must be based on the observation of external phenomena: it must be based on sense-data without reference to the divine or indeed to any preconceived *a priori* ideas. The second is that it concluded that in order to reduce the data obtained from the observation of external phenomena to a coherent and reliable system of knowledge they must be submitted to the discipline of mathematics. A recapitulation and further elaboration of the theories of two of the leading exponents of this revolution, Francis Bacon and René Descartes, will illustrate what is implied in this.

Bacon's intention, we noted,[44] was to provide a frame of reference for the whole range of physical phenomena, if not for all knowledge. All possible knowledge must be coordinated, he wrote, into 'a single systematic treatise, a Natural History such as may supply an orderly foundation for philosophy and include material reliable, abundant and well-arranged for the task of interpretation.'[45] But in order for such a task to be carried out there must be a complete separation of religion from 'philosophy': they must not be 'commixed together',[46] because while philosophy follows the light of nature (that is to say, is based upon experiment and observation) religion 'is grounded upon the Word and Oracle of God.'[47] Not only must no metaphysical or theological ideas provide the criteria for assessing the significance of what is observed, but also what is observed must not be thought to provide any evidence or support for metaphysical or theological ideas: 'out of the contemplation of nature to induce any verity or persuasion concerning the points of faith is in my judgement not safe.'[48] The divorce between religion and philosophy is absolute: concern for the spiritual is banished from the study of physical phenomena and all scientific knowledge must be derived from the observation of a natural world regarded as a self-subsistent entity.

Descartes comes in a somewhat different way to much the same conclusion, but with him the emphasis that the knowledge of nature is ultimately a mathematical knowledge is more explicit. This is not the place to retrace the steps by which Descartes arrived at his conclusion, 'I think, therefore I am'—a purely artificial conclusion, because one cannot think without thinking about something; or to retrace the steps by which, having established this initial certainty of self as the basis of thought, he went on to distinguish between ideas that were vague and confused and others that were clear and distinct and to accept the latter as being true apprehensions of and truly applicable to the real world. In this context I wish only to recall that Descartes was a great mathematician and that it was therefore perhaps inevitable that among these clear and distinct ideas which he accepted as true he regarded mathematical ideas as the most important. Mathematical ideas were true in a supreme sense, and it was they that could be taken as providing real knowledge.

This idealising attitude towards mathematics as providing real knowledge, or a knowledge of the real, was not of course new. It was the attitude, for instance, of the Greeks of the Pythagorean-Platonic tradition. But here it is important to make a distinction. Greek mathematics had no point of contact with sense-data. On the contrary it was held in high esteem precisely because it was thought to provide a way of escape from the physical world. It was seen as a way through which we could learn to leave the world of sense-data behind. In fact, it was because the phenomenal and historical world did not correspond to the ideal of mathematical knowledge that it came to be regarded as more or less unreal. What was real was the realm of entities which could be apprehended by the mind without the interposition of sense; and this realm of reality was changeless and timeless in the sense of having no reference to the world of change and time at all. Moreover, the geometrical figures in which it could be expressed were related to one another not physically but only intelligibly or logically. Hence in the Greek thought of this tradition there is a sharp divide between Being—which is the real world of the basically mathematical entities that constitute true knowledge—and Becoming, which is the phenomenal world of change and about which there can be no true knowledge but only opinion.

For Bacon and for Descartes on the other hand it was precisely this phenomenal world—the world of nature—that was the centre of interest. It was this world which by now was being regarded as virtually the real world, and as the basis of all knowledge—something that Descartes makes completely clear in the third of his four precepts of Logic, where he resolves 'to conduct my thoughts in such order that, by commencing with objects the simplest and easiest to know, I might ascend, little by little and, as it were, step by step, to the knowledge of the more complex.'[49] And if this more complex knowledge was assumed to have pre-eminently a mathematical character, so that mathematical knowledge was held to be the most perfect form of knowledge, this was for a reason more or less opposite to that for which it had been held in such high esteem by the Greeks of the Pythagorean-Platonic tradition: it was valued by the Cartesians precisely because it was thought that it corresponded to or was correlated with the phenomenal world of change and time, the world of sense-data.

In fact it was now believed that mathematics, and mathematics alone, could provide the most adequate account of the physical world. What this meant was that the experimental method, originally devised in order to assist in the discovery of the efficient causes of observed effects, now became a method of constructing mathematical descriptions of them which are thought to be true in their own right. The mathematical entities contained in the theories used to describe the 'appearances' are taken to be identical with the substance itself of the real world. They are given an ontological value in their own right. For Descartes and his successors, mathematics was not only the study of the world extended in time and space. It was also held to provide a real knowledge of this world. And mathematics, whether concerned with measurement or enumeration, is the application of the science of quantity.

Hence as a result of the scientific revolution of the seventeenth century it came to be thought not only that the world of nature is a self-contained entity, but also that those aspects of its reality which can be known in a true sense and which therefore alone have significance are those susceptible to mathematical or quantitative study and treatment. They are those aspects which can be weighed and measured and numbered—aspects which to all intents and purposes are claimed to constitute the whole of the natural order. It is this conclusion that gives Cartesian and post-Cartesian science its particular character and explains why the realm of nature apart from the divine has in the end become identified with the realm of science, and why science itself has been identified with the techniques of weight and enumeration and measurement.

It is in the light of these developments that we can see more clearly how and in what sense the building of our modern secular world has involved the desanctification of nature. First, in order for modern science to come into existence nature had to be regarded as an object divorced from all ontological roots or participation in the non-physical realm of the divine. What was known as formal causation disappears and what is left is the purely mechanistic interpretation of matter, according to which matter contains in itself the efficient causes of its own observable processes.

Second, the attribution of value and significance solely to those aspects of the natural order which are susceptible to quantitative study means that what was identified as nature was the realm of matter deprived of all qualitative elements, for the simple reason first that no non-observable qualities were to be taken into account and second that in any case no qualitative elements are susceptible to the kind of observation and analysis which science has adopted and which is, in an inexplicably exclusive manner, called scientific. Hence all spiritual qualities are *ipso facto* excluded from the objects science investigates, and at the same time it is tacitly assumed that there is nothing else to know about these objects except what can be observed by the so-called scientific method.

Physical phenomena are to be accounted for in physical categories alone, and that is all there is to be accounted for in them. The idea that every natural effect has a spiritual cause is completely neglected, and the fact that the neglect amounts to a kind of spiritual castration of the natural order seems to be of little or no concern. It is as if one examined and analyzed the Eucharist according to the scientific method and because one could not discern any trace of the divine in it declared that it was simply composed of its material elements. Having adopted a method of investigation which in its nature precludes the perception of spiritual qualities, it is gratuitous, to say the least, to pronounce that the object one investigates is to be explained in non-spiritual categories alone.

Yet it is the conclusions achieved by this kind of circulatory reasoning which for the last three hundred years or more have been regarded as constituting knowledge in a virtually exclusive sense and which moreover have been termed scientific. It is precisely the fact that these conclusions or what are called scientific theories are the product of this kind of circulatory reasoning, and not of experiment and observation, which makes the claim that they are objective so spurious. Having restricted the scope of scientific investigation to the rationally observable and purely quantitative aspects of what is changing and impermanent, and having adopted more or less exclusively a view of causality that takes into account merely efficient causes and ignores formal or spiritual causes, scientists are literally condemned to trying to explain things in terms of those meagre interpretative possibilities which are all they can now envisage. In other words, their theories or hypotheses do no more than reflect the limitations within which they operate and have no greater objectivity than the arbitrary and illusory assumptions which underlie them.

Modern science, then, ignoring the sacred aspect of nature as a condition of its own genesis and development, tries to fill the vacuum it has created by producing mathematical schemes whose only function is to help us to manipulate and 'dominate' matter on its own plane, which is that of quantity alone.[50] The physical world, regarded as so much dead stuff, becomes the scene of man's uncurbed exploitation for purely practical, utilitarian or acquisitive ends. It is treated as a de-incarnate world of phenomena that are without interest except in so far as they subserve statistics or fill test-tubes in order to satisfy the curiosity of the scientific mind, or are materially useful to man considered as a two-legged animal with no destiny beyond his earthly existence.

This is why the application of science—which is not really the application of science at all but the application of an unbelievable ignorance—has produced such disequilibrium, ugliness and even destruction not only in the natural world but in human life as well. Paradoxical as it may seem, through our attempt to achieve a knowledge of the world based on the observation of the physical phenomena of this world, we have reduced ourselves to a chronic state of blindness. We have lost our capacity to see not only the reality of the world about us but even of what was to have been the main purpose of our investigation to start with—the reality of our own presence within the world. If man thinks and acts as if God does not exist and is not present in all things, he thinks and acts a lie; and the result of this is that he reduces his own life to a falsity, which is the same thing as unreality.

As we have said, this dehumanization of man is an inevitable consequence of man's attempt to live as though he were only human. Man can be truly human only when he is mindful of his theomorphic nature. When he ignores the divine in himself and in other existences he becomes sub-human. And when this happens not merely in the case of a single individual but in the case of society as a whole, then that society disintegrates through the sheer rootlessness of its own structure or through the proliferation of psychic maladies which it is powerless to heal because it has deprived itself of the one medicine capable of healing them.[51]

Much of this has already been stated and there is no need to dwell on it here. Moreover, it must be said that many scientists themselves are now aware of it. They have begun to realise that by restricting science to the quantitative study of things they are imposing purely artificial limits on it and that so long as this is the case there can never be any understanding of the true nature of the objects they study: science under these conditions is forced to remain within the world of 'pointer-readings' and mathematical concepts which are no more than mere hypotheses, or which indeed may not have any reference to the real at all. They are fully aware too that since qualitative or spiritual elements are not subject to verification by the senses, no amount of experimental research can either prove or disprove their presence in the physical world. But it has seemed worthwhile to recall, however briefly, the main characteristics of

Cartesian and post-Cartesian science for two reasons, the one connected indirectly and the other directly with our theme.

The first reason is that while many scientists themselves have become aware of the impasse into which they have been led by science as conceived and practised in the post-Cartesian period, and so have also become conscious that perhaps therefore the assumptions on which that science is based need re-examination, Christian—as well as non-Christian—theologians often seem strangely unaware of all this. Indeed, we have developed, really in imitation of scientific practice, such disciplines as Biblical criticism or the historical method, and we are ready to 'de-mythologize' religion in the same imitative spirit; but we have singularly failed (with the exception of representatives of the Neo-Thomist school and one or two others) to provide any adequate criticism of modern science itself and of the assumptions on which it is based.

In fact, the contrary is more nearly the case: theologians and even human intelligence itself have capitulated to science. To understand the truth of this statement one has only to take into account the degree to which theologians accept the hypothesis of evolution, for instance, as axiomatic, and treat it as a kind of imperative condition to which everything, including theology itself, must accommodate itself. Teilhard de Chardin may be an extreme example of the capitulation of the religious consciousness to this hypothesis, but he is not alone by any means. Some even go so far as to regard the scientific method as a means which can be used in order to get a better understanding of the wisdom of God and the wonder of creation. In this view, the physicist who observes new patterns in the natural order and the technologist who applies these discoveries for practical purposes are both, whatever their attitude, fulfilling a 'high priestly' function, revealing and extending God's glory in the universe.

Indeed, nearly all attempts to reconcile religion and science have been made by theologians, not by scientists (who appear to be more perceptive in this respect). What such a reconciliation generally involves is an attempt to adapt the principles of religion—transcendent and immutable—to the latest findings of science, and so to make religion 'reasonable' or in keeping with the 'spirit of the age' by appearing 'scientific'. Naturally, the particular scientific hypotheses in the name of which this adaptation is carried out are often discarded by scientists them- selves by the time the theologians have completed their task. As has been pointed out, there can be no greater disservice done to the Christian religion than to tie it up with scientific views which in their very nature are merely temporary.[52] Far from religion and science mutually supporting each other it may be said that the more one is involved with science and its methods the more likely is one to become impervious to the experience of those realities which give religion its meaning. This is one reason why it has seemed worthwhile to point once again to the grounds which justify such a statement.

More important in this context is the second reason for indicating the main characteristics of post-Cartesian science and the manner in which it has so devastatingly contributed to the desanctification of the natural order. It is that these charac- teristics and their consequences are implicit in certain forms of the Christian theological tradition itself. An alleged connection between Christianity and modern science has often been affirmed. 'I am convinced', wrote Berdiaev,[53] 'that Christ- ianity alone made possible both positive science and technics'. Behind this kind of assumption is the idea that because the central proposition of Christianity is that 'The Logos was made flesh' it tends to be the most materialistic of all the great religions and so somehow the progenitor of the natural and materialist sciences.

This is as it may be, and in any case begs many questions. But whether there is some truth in it or not, it surely cannot be said that the aim of any religion is to produce a world from which nearly every non-material consideration is excluded, in which everything is seen as independent of God and in which it is claimed that things may be understood virtually as though God does not exist. One wonders whether the greatest deceit of the devil may not lie in his pretence to an independence of this kind. Yet it is precisely such an independent world—one in which the sacramental quality of things has been almost totally obscured—that has grown out of the western Christian matrix.

This may be in some part due to the character of Christianity itself and to the historical conditions in which it appeared. One might, for instance, in this connection point to the early Christian reaction against paganism, against the cosmic religion and the naturalism of the Hellenistic world, with its tendency to divinize the natural and human orders in their own right: a reaction expressed in Colossians[54] where the entire cosmos is described as controlled by 'the elemental spirits of the universe' opposed to Christ, although 'created through him and for him'. It has even been said that one of the most characteristic novelties of Christianity was that it demystified or, if you wish, secularized the cosmos: the idea that God abides in the elements, in water, in springs, in stars, in the emperor, was from the beginning totally rejected by the Apostolic Church;[55] and a legacy of this attitude is still evident in the horrified cry of 'pantheism' which tends to greet every suggestion that God does live in His creation. It may in this connection be relevant to point out here that what distinguishes the sacramental view of nature from a point of view which tends to divinize the natural order in its own right, is that while in the first nature is sought and known in the light of God, in the second it is God who is sought and identified in the elements of nature themselves.

Then in addition to this is the fact that Christianity is a religion without a sacred law. Unlike Judaism or Islam or Hinduism it possesses no *corpus* of concrete laws inseparable from its revelation and theoretically applicable to all aspects of human life and human society. It came as a spiritual way without such a *corpus*, so that when it became the religion of a civilization it was forced to incorporate Roman and even common law into its structure—law for which, in spite of the efforts of St Thomas and others, it was difficult to claim the authority of the will of God or the divine sanction possessed by the teachings of Christ which are concerned with direct spiritual principles. This has meant that it has always been more easy to detach, so to speak, the political, social and economic sphere of human life from the framework of the Christian revelation and so to leave it exposed to domination by purely secular interests and influences, than has been the case in the context of the civilizations of other great religions possessing a sacred law supported by the authority of revelation itself.

This being said, however, it still remains true that there is a direct causal connection between the process of desanctification of the natural order and certain developments within Christian theology itself. It is not posible here to do more than indicate the character of these developments. But if it is remembered that a recognition of the sacramental principle depends upon an understanding that in the sacrament there is an actual participation of the material in the spiritual, the created in the uncreated, so that the apparent ontological disparity between them is somehow transcended, then it follows that a failure to perceive the sacramental quality of the natural order must go with a failure to grasp this participation in all its fullness. It must go, in other words, with a sense that there is a virtually unbridgeable ontological gap between the spiritual and the material, the uncreated and the created. This would indicate that the theological developments in question would be those that tend to emphasize the disparity between the uncreated and the created realms and so lead to the one being regarded as independent of the other in the manner indicated.

The attempt to discern these developments may well begin with St Augustine. Here it must be said that what St Augustine in the first instance understands by nature is not the physical world as we now perceive it by means of the senses. Nature signifies for him first of all the original and uncontaminated state of things as they issued 'in the beginning' from God through the act of divine creation: the world before the Fall, before it became warped and depraved through human defection. But even here, in his conception of the creation of this pre-fallen world, and moreover in his conception of the creation of its highest and most perfect beings, the angels, St Augustine already inserts the thin end of the wedge which, driven further in, produces the sense of dichotomy between the uncreated and the created to which I have referred.

The quality of grace, St Augustine asserts—the quality of spiritual illumination—is not something intrinsic to the created nature of angels as such. It is not their natural element. It is something added to them as a gift. This giving presupposes the existence of a recipient. It presupposes the existence of a creature existing in a state other than that of grace. In other words, in the Augustinian perspective one is invited to envisage a historical phase in which the creature exists in a state of pure nature without participation in divine grace; and this is so even though both the creation of a being capable of receiving the gift of grace and the giving of the gift that is to be received are gratuitous acts on the part of God.

Moreover, according to St Augustine all created beings—angels and all beneath the angels—are first made (though not created) in the eternal uttering of their ideas in the Logos of God. But these ideas of things as they are in God's mind—these 'principial forms or stable and unchangeable essences of things', as St Augustine calls them[56]—in the light of which all things are created, again in Augustinian thought are not regarded as intrinsic to those things when they are created. They remain extrinsic to their being. They cannot become the core itself of that being, a ray of divine light within the creature. In themselves, created things must always remain distinct and separate from God ontologically. Rational creatures—angels and men—may apprehend themselves through intellection as ideas in God's mind. These ideas can be the standards for what each thing ought to be. But they can never become the reality itself of each thing, its own proper subject. The being of each thing in itself is and must remain exterior to the divine idea in the light of which it is created. It can never participate in the inner life of this idea.

The separation between Creator and created here appears as radical—a separation not to be bridged by any process of human thought or imagination or by any act of human will: any aspirations towards 'deification' in the traditional Christian sense are by definition chimerical, as is any attempt to see and know the divine through sharing in the life of the divine itself. What man can see or know of God are merely the *vestigia Dei* or traces of the divine visible in creation or impressed on the human mind by the source of divine light which itself must always remain exterior to it.[57]

This, as I said, is the state of affairs in the pre-fallen world. In the fallen world as seen by St Augustine—the world in which we actually live—things are far worse, and this separation between the uncreated and the created is now truly abysmal. Through the Fall man and the rest of the natural order are deprived of even that extrinsic participation in grace which they possessed in their pre-fallen state. Their original and true nature is now vitiated, totally corrupt and doomed to destruction. It is a lump of damnation.

As for the communication of grace, through which alone man and the world may be redeemed from depravity, this, it was thought by St Augustine and his mediaeval successors, was confined to the visible Church and depended on the performance of certain rites, like baptism, confirmation, ordination and so on, which it was the privilege of the ecclesiastical hierarchy to administer to a submissive and obedient laity. The magnificent scope of the Logos doctrine with its whole 'cosmic' dimension—the idea of God incarnate in all human and created existence—which from the time of the Alexandrians and Cappadocians down to the present day has been one of the major themes of Orthodox Christian theology, was tacitly but radically constricted in Western thinking. Spontaneous personal participation 'in Christ' became identified with membership of a juristic corporational institution which claimed to be the unique sphere of the Spirit's manifestation, the judge of His presence, and the manipulator of His activity.

In these conditions to say that everything in the created order by virtue of the simple fact of its existence possesses, even if unaware of it and so in a potential state, an intrinsically sacramental quality which unites it to the divine, would have been tantamount to blasphemy. Instead, there was a radical separation of the sacred from the secular: everything inside the Church (understood as an earthly society) was sacred; outside the formal limits of the Church, or in nature, the activity of the Spirit was denied: everything outside these limits was secular, deprived of grace, incurably corrupt and doomed to disintegration.

From St Augustine we may turn to the other major representative of western mediaeval theology, St Thomas Aquinas; and it is against this background of the radical disparity in St Augustine's thought between the world and the Church, nature and grace, or nature and what is now regarded as the supernatural, that the efforts of St Thomas to 'save' the natural world must be viewed. Unless it is viewed against this background the fact that his thought helped to consolidate the rift between the world of nature and the divine and so contributed to the process of desanctification we are tracing may seem inexplicable.

It must be remembered that by the time St Thomas set out upon his attempt to reconcile all views, however contradictory they might appear, in an all-embracing synthesis, the idea of the separation between the natural (understood now in the non-Augustinian, Aristotelian sense as a physical reality) and the supernatural was so deeply embedded in Latin thought that it was impossible to establish any genuine ontological link between them. The only way therefore by which the natural world could be freed from the opprobrium attached to it in Augustinian thought and could be accorded a positive status in its own right was, paradoxical as it may sound, to dissociate it altogether from the sphere of theology, to make it independent of theological control, and to substitute for any genuine relationship between the sphere of nature and the sphere of theology the principle of analogy.

It was to this end that St Thomas made his suggestion that there are two levels on which things are viewable, the natural and the supernatural level. The latter is the state in which grace is paramount, and it corresponds to the sphere of theology. But where the efficacy of nature itself is concerned, no grace is necessary, because nature follows its own inherent laws which have nothing to do with grace.[58] All grace does in relation to the natural world is to bring to perfection the operations in nature which have begun without its intervention and exist quite independently of it: grace does not destroy nature but perfects it,[59] and this is to imply that although nature is better with the addition of grace it can exist quite adequately without it.

The immediate conclusion is that there must be different principles appertaining to the natural and the supernatural spheres. There must be, as St Thomas put it,[60] a double order in things. This means that nature itself—the natural as such—is now accorded a status of its own, to all intents and purposes independent of the divine; and the Augustinian dichotomy between nature and grace is replaced by a dualism between the natural and the supernatural. Assuredly, God is still regarded as the author of nature, but essentially nature works according to its own laws, and it is quite sufficient to take account only of these laws in order to discover how nature does work.

Moreover, these laws are thought to be characterized by reasonableness or rationality; and man, defined now as a rational animal, shares in the laws of nature to the fullest extent because he can recognize them through his reasoning faculties. This natural reasoning capacity with which man is endowed operates without any revelation or grace and may pursue its investigations without any reference to the articles of faith. Indeed, the only knowledge which man as a rational creature could effectively obtain was said to be that which he could derive from the observation of phenomena through the senses[61]—a proposition which is at the very basis of the later scientific attitude to knowledge.

It is true that St Thomas was constrained to state that the conclusions of natural reason could not affect, and must ultimately conform to, the conclusions of faith. But he was constrained to state this because God Himself—and this is the lynch-pin of the whole system—was now regarded as to the fullest degree a rational being, so that unless something had gone very wrong somewhere there could hardly be any ultimate contradiction between the principles of God's rationality and the laws of nature which He had established to operate on purely rational lines. By means of this kind of argument St Thomas was able to preserve a delicate and correspondingly precarious synthesis between the idea that nature was an integral part of the divine order and the idea that essentially it existed in its own right, autonomous and independent within its own terms of reference, operating according to its own laws, premisses and purposes.

Analytical Thomist methodology, with its supposition that man is dependent on sense-data for the acquisition of knowledge and that he can apprehend spiritual realities only in so far as he discerns in the natural world evidence of their transcendent and unknowable perfections,[62] effectively promotes the idea that there is an uncrossable boundary between God and man, between the divine and the human. Implicit in it is a failure to grasp the full significance of the unity of the two natures in one person; and the immediate consequence of this was to be the neglect of the possibility of man's personal participation in the divine and a growth in the conviction that he may know the truth concerning God only indirectly by means of his rational faculty operating within the one sphere accessible to it, that of the natural world. And here again what is implicit is not man's supra-rational and personal participation in the inner meaning, the indwelling *logos* of this world, or his disclosure of God's self-expression within it, but a belief that he may decipher, articulate and eventually dominate it as a self-sufficient entity by the use of his individual reason in disregard of, if not in contradiction to, the truths of the Christian revelation.

The result could only be that in the following centuries philosophers (like for instance William of Ockham or Marsiglio of Padua) less endowed than St Thomas with a capacity for maintaining his subtle balance between nature and revelation, would break the now tenuous link between nature and the divine, would assert the autonomy of reason, divorce philosophy completely from religion, and claim an unlimited charter to pursue their own methods of inquiry into nature without any reference to metaphysical or theological principles, not because God did not exist or had not created nature but because in practical terms He was no longer present as an immanent, ever-working principle and energy in the natural world.

The scene was set for the scientific revolution of the seventeenth century and the emergence of the mechanistic and materialist science of the modern world; and it is not without justice that in a famous passage Alfred North Whitehead traces the origin of the modern scientific movement directly back to the scholastic insistence on the rationality of God and to the concomitant insistence, reached in the way we have described, on the belief that every detailed occurrence in the physical world can be correlated with its antecedents in a perfectly definite and rational manner.[63]

That in trying to rescue nature from the pit of perdition to which it had been consigned by St Augustine, St Thomas should have contributed in this way directly to the formation of the secular mentality and secular approach to nature does, as I said, become understandable when it is remembered that he accepted as virtually axiomatic the conception of a God who by definition cannot be ontologically present in the activities of the world which He has created. But the question remains as to why the presence of God is thought to be limited in this way, and it is in answering this question that it may be possible to specify the limitations of the Augustinian-Thomist tradition more precisely. I would venture to suggest that the answer to this question is related to two interconnected themes, the one metaphysical and the other theological.

The metaphysical theme is connected with a conception of form and matter, basically Aristotelian in character but accepted by both St Augustine and St Thomas, according to which God is identified with the formal and active principle and matter is regarded as the principle of formlessness and potentiality. This latter principle, although not opposed explicitly to God, is said to have an absolutely minimal degree of being, and is to such an extent identified with non-being in a purely privative or deficient sense that it can be described as that which is not.[64] In fact, its capacity to be is limited to a capacity to receive form, which comes solely from God, while in itself it tends always, by its formlessness, towards nothingness and non-existence.[65] In short, it is the abyss of disintegration over which every created being is suspended, and as such it is linked with evil, which in its turn may be equated with a disruption of form or a perversity of order, a lapse into non-being.[66]

Moreover, this material principle of formlessness is said to lie at the basis of all formal creation: everything created is regarded as a mixture or composition of matter with form, of an indeterminate substratum with the determination acquired from God. Hence no finite being can ever be 'like' God, still less be 'deified', because by definition all finite beings share in the material substratum with its intrinsic deficiency and 'godlessness'. God—the formal principle and the principle of Being—is pure actuality and there is no potentiality in Him. The material principle on the other hand, which is a formless or deficient cause, coincides with potentiality. Since natural existence also shares in the character of potentiality it can never be a sacramental reality in the full sense of the word unless it becomes other than it is or is, in other words, transubstantiated.

One of the limitations in the Augustinian-Thomist tradition which would appear to make it difficult, if not impossible, to envisage a full and reciprocal union between God and nature, the uncreated and the created, is therefore that God is conceived solely as the principle of pure actuality, with the consequence that potentiality is regarded as implying a certain lack of being in a negative or deficient sense and so in this respect as outside God; and the same must apply to whatever shares in potentiality.

The theological theme in which a certain limitation in this same tradition is expressed is connected with the doctrine of the Trinity. Here perhaps we reach what is really the crux of the matter. The sacramental understanding of nature depends, as we have seen, upon the recognition of the actual immanence of nature in the divine, the sense that the creative energies of God did not merely produce the created world from without like a builder or an engineer, but are the ever-present, indwelling and spontaneous causes of every manifestation of life within it, whatever form this may take. It depends, in other words, upon the recognition of the continuing, vitalizing activity of the Holy Spirit in the world, animating these energies—luminous uncreated radiations of the divine—in the very heart of every existing thing. In its essence therefore the absence of this sacramental understanding must signify a deficiency in the doctrine of the Holy Spirit.

In effect, the doctrine of the Holy Spirit was not fully affirmed in Latin Christendom. The 'cosmic' significance of Pentecost, in which the revelation of the Father and Son is consummated in that of the Spirit, was attenuated, and the full deployment of the doctrine of the Trinity was correspondingly arrested and frozen.[67] The Son was conceived pre-eminently in the unity of His being with that of the Father; and this emphasis on the transcendent unity and simplicity of the Trinity, confirmed and sealed by the *filioque*, meant that the Spirit was regarded as in ontological dependence on the Son. This in its turn, combined with a failure to distinguish adequately between God's essence and His existence or, in the case of St Thomas, with a conception that actually identifies God's essence with His existence, prevented it from being possible to understand how God, in the Spirit, 'goes out' of Himself and enters with His uncreated 'existential' energies into creation without either disrupting His unity and simplicity or abandoning His transcendence.

Under these conditions it was of course impossible to visualize any real activity of the Spirit in nature or, conversely, any real participation of nature in the divine. Instead nature, in the way we have seen, is accorded a status of its own, independent of the divine. And the same status is accorded to man, because man, defined as a rational animal, shares in all the characteristics and attributes of nature. It only remained for the now tenuously-conceived link between the divine and nature, the divine and the human, to be broken—not by denying that God created both nature and man but by saying that for all practical purposes the divine cannot be taken into account as an operational principle—and the way was open for that process of dehumanization and desanctification to which our contemporary world bears such powerful witness.

Epilogue

CAN WE OVERCOME this process of dehumanization and desanctification? We cannot know. But we can at least point to certain conditions on whose fulfilment depends our survival as human beings. The first is that, however perilous our situation, we do not on that account regard it as inevitable that we are doomed and that there is no alternative except progressive materialization leading to the Armageddon and the coming of the Anti-Christ. One of the great dangers is precisely that we become spell-bound before the sphinx-like monster of the world we have brought into existence. We even forget that it is we who have produced it, not it which has produced us. In this way we are reduced to a kind of helpless passivity, lamenting the world of natural simplicities and sacred forms that has gone, and seeing in the present and the immediate future the necessary and inescapable declension of the cosmic cycles into a pre-ordained dark age ending in the emergence of the beast from the abyss. We commit a kind of apostasy. We surrender to the image of negation and purposelessness which we are summoned to overcome.

We surrender in fact to what is the most negative and ugly side of our nature. Certainly we must realize that the scope and purpose of the modern scientific and technological mentality are at the opposite pole to the Christian scope and purpose of transfiguring all human and natural life through prayer, sanctity and loving compassion; and that not only can there be no reconciliation between these two orientations, but also that the pursuit of the first may well erase the significance of the second from our minds. But such erasure is not simply an automatic and inevitable matter. If it happens, it is because we allow it to happen. It is only man himself who can consent to the damning of his own soul, and nothing and no one can force him to give this consent, least of all the machine and other abstract and technical processes.

If we cannot see how to restore the traditional forms of a Christian society, or to be the type of man of the ages of faith, we do not because of that cease to be created in the image and likeness of God, or lose our capacity to realize this image and likeness in our personal lives. We demean our own dignity when we attribute either a final character to the present scientific and technological period, or regard it as fatally and necessarily leading to our own human and terrestrial deformation or extinction. It may well lead to this. But, it must be repeated, if it does, this is our own responsibility. We are faced with a challenge, an issue of life or death: either to affirm the eternal nature of our being—that image in us and the values that go with it which lie beyond all forms of society, whatever their character—or to acquiesce in our own dehumanization and eclipse in obedience to the forces that with our cooperation have fabricated the infernal and artificial forms of the contemporary world.

If, though, we choose not to acquiesce, then we must realize that the first step towards becoming disentangled from these forms is the step of repentance, or *metanoia*: change of mind. Such a conclusion must follow from all that has been said in this book. The thesis of the book has been that the forms of our society, from those of our educational system down to those in which most of us spend our working lives, are such that they frustrate and even negate the expression and fulfilment of our true humanity at practically every turn. But as it is the pursuit of the ideals and methods of modern science that has brought us into this catastrophic situation, clearly there can be no issue from it without the renunciation of these ideals and methods. We have to free ourselves from subservience to the type of mentality by which we have been increasingly dominated over the last three or four centuries.

This mentality is the mentality which has produced modern science; and we have to realize that scientists are specialists who within the confines of their specialities may possess a capacity for order and sense of a formidable kind but who outside these confines produce disorder and nonsense which are equally formidable. This is because the conceptual ground within which knowingly or unknowingly they think and act does not permit anything else. As we have already said, modern scientific thought has no complexity or depth whatsoever. It does not even acknowledge the crucial distinction between the order of wisdom and the order of mere hypothesis based on experiment. It proceeds with blind determination from the premises that underpin it to the conclusions that inevitably follow from those premises. It demonstrates the efficacy of these conclusions by totally ignoring their human and ecological consequences. Its attempts to justify the premises themselves in terms of value and to say that they are 'good' are little more than extrapolations from its capacity to analyse and describe, in the most superficial manner, what works and how it works.

At the same time this experimental mentality protects itself from the disruption with which it is threatened by every form of knowledge less shallow than its own by building around itself the departmental structure of modern schools and universities and by securing the undivided allegiance of corporate industrialists, bankers, big businessmen, and the clients of these people, the politicians and officials of the modern state system. In this sense it is monolithic and potentially totalitarian, aspiring to a monopoly that will permit experimentally derived, technologically pure solutions to be imposed by force. To think and act without the constraint of any knowledge and values other than those of the modern scientific mentality is to commit oneself to a tyranny of an unprecedented maleficence. That is why the freeing of ourselves from subservience to this mentality constitutes the second condition whose fulfilment is a prerequisite of our survival as human beings.

Does this mean that there cannot be either any science of phenomena or any practical technology based upon such a science? This does not follow at all. But if the consequences of the pursuit of such a science are to be the fostering and not the destruction of our humanity, several things have to be recognized. The first is that knowledge and what is done under the influence of a particular form of knowledge can never in the nature of things be neutral. For knowledge is either true knowledge, based on a true recognition of the reality of things, or it is false knowledge, based on a mistaken idea of the reality of things. But if it is false knowledge it is also on that account a diabolic form of knowledge, the product of 'the father of lies', and hence it is tainted with evil. Consequently what is done under its influence is likewise tainted with evil.

This means, in the context with which we are here concerned, that if a science of phenomena starts out, as modern science does start out, with a mistaken idea of the relationship between the divine and the human, or the divine and nature, or, quite simply, with no awareness of the divine at all, the conclusions it reaches as to the nature of both man and the natural world will necessarily be false and to that extent diabolic; and all that is implemented, whether by way of educational programmes or of technology, under the influence of such a diabolic form of knowledge will be tainted with the same character. As such it will inescapably be destructive of both man and nature, however neutral it may appear to be. As modern science as a whole has developed on the basis of such false premises, its so-called knowledge is a false knowledge and its consequences in the sphere of practical application are therefore inevitably destructive.

Yet it is by no means itself inevitable that a science of phenomena or a practical technology based on it should develop from false premisses—should develop, that is to say, from a mistaken idea of who man is or of the relationship between the divine and the natural worlds. Consequently it is by no means inevitable that the findings of such a science or their practical application should be destructive of both man and nature. But for a science of phenomena not to be based on false premisses requires on the part of scientists themselves a double act of recognition: first, the recognition that the conceptual framework within which modern science has been and still is operating is a false one and that this has the inescapable consequences we have noted in the practical sphere; and, second, the recognition that there can be no true knowledge of the physical world that does not derive from an *a priori* acceptance of a metaphysical knowledge—of a metaphysical knowledge which it is quite impossible to attain through the investigation, in however subtle or sophisticated a form, of the phenomenal world itself.

In other words, for a science of phenomena not to be false and destructive, its theory and practice must be based on an *a priori* acceptance of ideas as to the ultimate and intrinsic nature of reality which derive from a religious or metaphysical tradition. This is to say that they have to be based on the recognition and assimilation of ideas whose origin lies not in the human mind but in the mind of God as this has been disclosed to man through revelation. Such recognition and assimilation will always elude us until and unless we raise our consciousness above the level of the reason, because in themselves the categories of the reason exclude the possibility of attaining a metaphysical knowledge. Without such knowledge—knowledge capable of providing a bridge linking the human and the divine —the reason merely formulates endless hypotheses that involve us ever more disastrously in the world of materialization and illusion.

The third and overriding condition of our survival as human beings is, then, the recognition that the primordial ideas of a religious or metaphysical tradition must constitute the conceptual framework within which a science of phenomena has to operate if it is not to result in a false knowledge and hence to have consequences that, instead of fostering, positively negate man's humanity and his ability to live in harmony with himself and the natural world. Indeed, one can go further and say quite simply that it is the recognition of such primordial ideas as the operative standards guiding not only science but every form of human activity that is the *sine qua non* of our survival as human beings and that without such a recognition we are inevitably doomed to a total deformation and even to extinction. This is the case because these primordial ideas are themselves the expression on the conceptual level of the divine principles in the image of which both man himself and the natural world are created. To align all forms of human activity with them is thus to ensure that one does not violate the norms of human and natural life; it is to prevent oneself from stepping over into those spheres of dehumanization and desanctification into which modern science, by ignoring the standards they establish, has stepped with a vengeance.

Yet if we are to recover an awareness of such ideas within the framework of the Christian tradition—and the thesis proposed in the opening chapter of the present study is that this is the only real possibility available to us who belong to the cultural orbit of the western world—we have to turn to the doctrinal masters of this tradition who have most clearly and authentically understood and expressed them. In the works of these masters—and again in the opening chapter we specified some of the most important of them—is enshrined the sole living heritage of spiritual wisdom which the western world possesses, obscured though it may be by the developments we have been discussing. Our ignorance of them is consequently a measure of the degree to which we have betrayed our inheritance, an inheritance common to the whole of Christendom. Concomitantly, if we are to overcome this ignorance, and to rediscover and reaffirm the true dignity of both man and nature in a way capable perhaps of stemming, if not of turning, the tide of progressive materialization and disintegration on which we are all now carried, it can only be by rediscovering and reaffirming the spiritual principles on which these masters have based their life and their thought.

Notes

1. For a full account of St Maximos's anthropology, see Lars Thunberg, *Microcosm and Mediator: The Theological Anthropology of Maximus the Confessor* (London, 1965). My own account of the same subject in this present chapter is indebted to this work.

2. On St Symeon the New Theologian, see G. A. Malone, S. J., *The Mystic of Fire and Light* (Denville, N. J., 1975); and on St Gregory Palamas, see J. Meyendorff, *Introduction à l'étude de Grégoire Palamas* (Editions du Seuil, Paris, 1959; abbreviated English translation 1964). For an authoritative introduction to this whole tradition, see V. Lossky, *The Mystical Theology of the Eastern Church* (London, 1957).

3. For an exemplification of this, see my *Church, Papacy and Schism* (London, 1978), pp.78-95.

4. Col. 1:15.

5. For an account of St Augustine's thought, see E. Gilson, *Introduction a l'etude de St Augustin* (Paris, 1931).

6. See below, Chapter 4, p.107ff.

7. For an introduction to this theme, see Sir David Ross, *Plato's Theory of Ideas* (Oxford, 1953).

8. For a detailed account of the Christology of the Greek patristic tradition, see Aloys Grillmeier, *Christ in Christian Tradition* (London, 1965) and John Meyendorff, *Christ in Eastern Christian Thought* (Washington, 1969). See also Lars Thunberg, *Microcosm and Mediator*, op. cit., pp.21-50.

9. See S. L. Frank, *Reality and Man* (London, 1965), p.134 in particular, but also Chapter IV as a whole, to which I am indebted for many insights connected with the present theme.

10. Gal. 2:20.

11. For references to this distinction between the intellect and the reason, and for the characterizations of the intellect which follow, see *Intellect* in the indexes to Vols. 1-3 of *The Philokalia* (London, 1979, 1981 and 1984).

12. St Maximos the Confessor, *Questiones ad Thalassium* (P.G. 90, 624 A). Cited p.217 of Hans Urs von Balthasar, *Liturgie Cosmique: Maxime le Confessor* (Paris, 1947).

13. Luke 9:3.

14. John 12:25.

15. Matthew 10:39; 16:25; Mark 8:25; Luke 1:9.

16. For a fuller exploration of this theme and of the sources here referred to, see C. E. Rolt, *The Spiritual Body* (London, 1920).

17. Or the author of the writings attributed to St Makarios.

18. For the idea of man as the microcosmos, see Rudolf Allers, 'Microcosmos from Anaximandros to Paracelsus', *Traditio* 2 (1944), pp.319-407.

19. See below, Chapter 4, p.107ff.

20. St Augustine, *In Joannis Evangelium*, 19, 5. 15. P.L. 35, 1553. On man as soul using body, see *De Moribus Ecclesiae*, 1, 27. 52. P.L. 32, 1332.

21. St Augustine, *De Trinitate*, xv.7.11; P.L. 42, 1065.

22. For a partial exploration, see E. Gilson, *Reason and Revelation in the Middle Ages* (New York, 1939), and his *The Philosophy of St. Thomas Aquinas* (Cambridge, 1924). See also A. C. Crombie, *Robert Grosseteste* (Oxford, 1953).

23. For a brief account of Aristotle's understanding of universals, see Sir David Ross, *Aristotle* (London, 1964), pp.157-159. See also H. Cherniss, *Aristotle's Criticism of Plato and the Academy* (New York 1962), passim.

24. See Sir David Ross, *Aristotle*, op. cit., pp.165-167.

25. See Anton C. Pegis, *At the Origins of the Thomistic Notion of Man* (New York, 1963).

26. See St Thomas Aquinas, *De Anima*, a.5; *De Unitate Intellectus* iv, 86; *De Spiritualibus Creaturis*, a.10.

27. See Joseph Pieper, *The Silence of St Thomas* (London, 1957), pp.63-65.

28. St Thomas Aquinas, *Commentaria in Librum Boethii De Trinitate*, 6,3. See below, Chapter 4, p.111ff.

29. St Thomas Aquinas, *De Spiritualibus Creaturis*, a.3.

30. St Thomas Aquinas, *Summa Theologica*, I, Qu. 76, art. I, ad. 6.

31. For an introduction to Descartes' thought, see Jacques Maritain, *Three Reformers* (London, 1928) and Henri Gouhier, *La Pensée Métaphysique de Descartes* (Paris, 1969).

32. See Jacques Ellul, *The Technological Society* (New York, 1964), pp.27 ff.

33. See below, Chapter 4, p.98ff.

34. See my article, 'Teilhard de Chardin and the Christian Vision', in *Studies in Comparative Religion*, Summer 1970, pp.150-175.

35. See Michael Polanyi, *Personal Knowledge* (New York, 1964), *passim* but particularly Chapter 10. See also Chaim Perelman, 'Polanyi's Interpretation of Scientific Inquiry', in *Intellect and Hope: Essays in the Thought of Michael Polanyi*, ed. T. A. Langford and W. H. Poteat (Duke University Press, 1968), pp.232-241.

36. See his *The Tao of Physics* (Berkeley, 1975) and his *The Turning Point* (London, 1982).

37. Joseph Needham, *Man a Machine* (London, 1927), p.93. Cited p.184 of T. Roszak, *Where the Wasteland Ends* (London, 1973), a book to which I am here indebted.

38. Francis Crick, *Of Molecules and Men* (University of Washington Press, 1966), pp.87, 93. Cited by T. Roszak, *Where the Wasteland Ends*, op. cit., p.188.

39. See below, Chapter 4, pp.104-5.

40. See below, Chapter 4, p.110ff.

41. See *A Holy Tradition of Working, Passages from the Writings of Eric Gill*, edited and introduced by Brian Keeble (Ipswich, 1983), and David Jones, *Epoch and Artist* (London, 1959).

42. This is the thesis of such writers as René Dubos in his *The Wooing of Earth* (New York, 1980). In Appendix III of this book he gives a relevant bibliography.

43. Cyril of Alexandria, P. G. 74, 564.

44. See above, Chapter 3, p.70.

45. Francis Bacon, Preface to *Parasceve*, in *The Works of Francis Bacon*, ed. J. Spedding, R. L. Ellis, D. D. Heath (London, 1889), p.393.

46. Francis Bacon, *Advancement of Learning*, ed. W. A. Wright (Oxford, 1900), II, 6, i.

47. Ibid, II, 24, 3.

48. Ibid, II, 6, i.

49. Descartes, *Discourse on Method*, 2, trans. J. Veitch, *The Method, Meditations and Selections from the Principles of Descartes* (London, 1899), p.19.

50. T. Burckhardt, 'Cosmology and Modern Science', *Tomorrow* (London, Summer 1964), p.186.

51. Seyyed Hossein Nasr, *The Encounter of Man and Nature* (London, 1968), passim.

52. E. Mascall, *Christian Theology and Natural Science* (London, 1956), p.166.

53. N. Berdiaev, *The Meaning of History* (London, 1935), p.113.

54. Col. 1:16; 2:8.

55. J. Meyendorff, 'Orthodox Theology Today', *Sobornost*, series 6, 1 (London, 1970), p.16.

56. St Augustine, *De Diversis Quaestionibus*, 83, 46, 1-2; P.L. 40, 29-30.

57. See E. TeSelle, 'Nature and Grace in Augustine's Expositions of Genesis I, 1-5', *Recherches augustiniennes*, V (Paris, 1968), pp.95-137.

58. St Thomas Aquinas, *Summa Theologica*, I-II, qu 10, art 1.

59. St Thomas Aquinas, *Summa Theologica*, I, i, qu 8, ad 2.

60. St Thomas Aquinas, *Summa Theologica*, I, qu 21, art 1 ad 3.

61. St Thomas Aquinas, *De Veritate*, ii, 3, obj 19 et ad 19; *Summa Theologica*, Ia, 12, 12.

62. St Thomas Aquinas, *Contra Gentiles*, I, 3.

63. A. N. Whitehead, *Science and the Modern World* (New York, 1926), p.18.

64. St Augustine, *Confessions*, XII, 6, 6.

65. St Augustine, *De Genesi ad litteram*, I, 4, 9.

66. See E. TeSelle, *Augustine the Theologian* (London, 1970), pp.143-4.

67. On this theme, see my *Church, Papacy and Schism*, op.cit., pp.96-114.

Index